# Endorsements

Having a source of light is vital, especially when our world seems to shudder in darkness. "We cannot know God as God is, and God knows that we cannot." Though we cannot know God fully, through reading the words of Walter Rauschenbusch, we can know more about who we are in God. We can discern more about how to live for God. We can come closer to God as revealed in the flesh. *Life with God* is a source of shimmering illumination. In its pages, wisdom and hope shine brightly. No matter our circumstances, we need not dwell in darkness. In this volume, the radiance of God awaits us through Rauschenbusch's wisdom and words. For all who will enter this volume, you will leave enriched, refreshed, and renewed.

Rev. Dr. Zina Jacque<br>
Alfred Street Baptist Church, Pastor for Small Groups (Emeritus)<br>
Alexandria, VA

We live in an era in which Christianity seems increasingly to be reduced to politics — either the politics we like, or the politics we don't like. This beautiful collection of brief spiritual meditations by Walter Rauschenbusch comes as a timely corrective indeed. Even Walter, who was as politically committed as any 20th century Christian leader, had a spiritual life that both grounded and transcended his political vision. He loved God, and he wanted others to love God. I highly recommend this collection.

Rev. Dr. David P. Gushee<br>
Distinguished University Professor of Christian Ethics, Mercer University<br>
Chair in Christian Social Ethics, Vrije Universiteit<br>
Elected Past-President, American Academy of Religion and<br>
Society of Christian Ethics

We owe Dennis Johnson a debt of gratitude for making Walter Rauschenbusch accessible to non-scholars. Dr. Johnson makes the case that one best becomes acquainted with characters via their own words, more than through words about them. Dr. Johnson gives us both. His biographical introduction tantalizes readers who haven't sufficient time to read Chris Evans' or Paul Minus' lengthy biographies. Through the excerpts and prayers selected for *Life with God* we have the opportunity to get to know Rauschenbusch through his own words. Dr. Johnson's own spirit of gentleness and desire to reflect Christlikeness shine through his work, and remind us of the timelessness of life with God.

Rev. Dr. Priscilla E. Eppinger
Executive Director, American Baptist Historical Society

Walter Rauschenbusch was genius in knowing the eternal in the midst of the cacophony of his own context. Dennis Johnson has performed an invaluable service for all those who want to know and follow Jesus by bringing Rauschenbusch's voice into the conversation with the cacophony of the context today. This book's organization is practical. It can be read meditatively straight through focused on the categories of Solitude, Service and Solidarity. Also it can be used topically for those seeking guidance on topics such as "re-establishing the teachings of Jesus," how confronting injustice in the structures of society leads to the revision of how one studies the Bible, recognizing that the "reign of fear is never the reign of God," or picturing solidarity as "putting our feet under the same table." Rauschenbusch is an inspiring guide to all those who would be molded by God's love for the whole of God's own creation instead of fear of the powers and principalities of the day.

Phyllis Rodgerson Pleasants Tessieri, PhD
John F. Loftis Professor of Church History (retired)

Dennis Johnson does the Church a gracious favor by reminding us of the conjunction that was Walter Rauschenbusch. Through this curation of prayers and writings from the unpublished or little known publishing of Rauschenbusch we see the connection between social justice and spirituality, scholarship and devotion, joy and lament, rest and renewal, private prayer and public action. Dear reader, read, mark, learn and inwardly digest these prayers and reflections as the way to socialize, tenderize and conscientize your soul.

Travis Norvell
Author and Pastor of Judson Memorial Baptist Church
Minneapolis, MN

A student of Rauschenbusch who was my social ethics professor in seminary first introduced me to Walter Rauschenbusch over 50 years ago. At that time, I knew nothing about Rauschenbusch and Hell's Kitchen in New York City, growing up in Boston. Reading his works completed my theology of the righteousness of God on earth. Our world today is as fractured and divided as any time in history that can be made whole and complete again when people of faith lead with their convictions into the "Hell's Kitchens" in the world today.

To appreciate the depth of the prayers and words of Rauschenbusch in this volume, the editor provides a poignant and honest portrayal of Rauschenbusch's life and in particular, his time during WWI. Labeling Rauschenbusch with "feet of clay," we come face to face with who he was; very much like us. Rauschenbusch's personal prayer life becomes the driving force to his social witness.

What make this volume richer still is that the introduction and perhaps the selected pieces in this book is as much as a reflection of Dennis Johnson's journey of faith to practice his faith both in words and deeds. To read this book is to hear from one of our Baptist heroes, to walk with one of our close clergy colleagues on the path, and to be open to listening to what God may be calling us to be and do in the revealing of the Reign of God.

Rev. Dr. Don Ng
Pastor (retired), First Chinese Baptist Church of San Francisco
Past President, American Baptist Churches USA

In these days it is important to consider the voices we choose to hear — the voices that will feed our souls. In *Life with God*, Johnson curates a moving collection of prayers that invite us to join a journey of challenge and fulfillment, while revealing Rauschenbusch as a gifted pastoral and spiritual guide.

Dr. David Cassady
President, BSK Theological Seminary
Lexington and Louisville, Kentucky

In our late-modern sensibilities we have too often separated the academy from the church and the lecture hall from the pulpit. We have assumed that for one to have the mind of a scholar one must lose the heart of a pastor. Dennis Johnson's book reminds us that this need not be the case for one of the great American thinkers, Walter Rauschenbusch. Johnson's careful curation of Rauschenbusch's devotional practices and writings reminds us that there are those who lived what they taught and fully embraced what they believed. This collection of prayers and poems offers today's reader a true devotional companion and an opportunity to be taught and pastored by one who truly loved and cared for all.

> Rev. Dr. Jonathan Malone
> Wilderness Pastor and Founder/Owner of Wilderness Journeys

Dennis Johnson invites us to discover what's been lost for so long in our dry academic analyses of Rauschenbusch — the beating heart of a pastor, the true soul of a movement, and the one God at their center. More than a devotional, *Life with God* is modern monasticism, a guide in our own walk with the Divine and a reminder that the best theology and the best theologians are those whose lives, as Rauschenbusch himself once prayed, are "aquiver with God."

> Rev. Dr. Jason A. Henschel
> Senior Pastor, Wyoming Baptist Church in Cincinnati, OH
> Review Editor, The American Baptist Quarterly

These writings of Walter Rauschenbusch arrived on a week when the world felt shaken and many were grasping for words to comfort and offer hope. These were the words I needed.

Poetic and profound, Rauschenbusch feels like a friend who understands the perplexities of change, has endured the turmoil of conflict, and finds the courage to not only admire the teachings of Jesus but to follow. Even titles of the poems, prayers, and writings are balm to the soul: Embrace the Good Things, Despite the Excesses; Seek, Yield, Keep Open, Press Onward; Commit You All that Grieves You. They draw the reader into the prayer that suffuses this generous and lovingly assembled collection: "We need you, O great enlarger of our souls…." Thank you, Dennis L. Johnson, for bringing a great gift of a prophetic and trustworthy leader of faith to our time of need.

> Rev. Dr. Heather Entrekin
> Retired American Baptist Minister

# Life with God

## Daily Reflections with Walter Rauschenbusch

Dennis L. Johnson
Foreword by Paul Raushenbush

© 2025
Published in the United States by Nurturing Faith, Macon, GA.
Nurturing Faith is a book imprint of Good Faith Media (goodfaithmedia.org).
Library of Congress Cataloging-in-Publication Data is available.

ISBN: 978-1-63528-249-8

All rights reserved. Printed in the United States of America.

Material from the Rauschenbusch Family Collection, RG 1003, is included in this volume courtesy of the American Baptist Historical Society, Atlanta, GA.

Unless otherwise indicated, Bible quotations in this volumed are from The New Revised Standard Version of the Bible (NRSV), copyright © 1989 by the Division of Christian Education of the National Council of Churches in Christ in the United States of America. Used by permission. All rights reserved.

Bible quotations marked "Montgomery" are from The New Testament in Modern English translated by Helen Barrett Montgomery © 1924 by American Baptist Publication Society. All rights reserved.

Bible quotations marked "Goodspeed" are from The New Testament: An American Translation translated by Edgar J. Goodspeed. The University of Chicago Press © 1923.

# Contents

Foreword.................................................................................................1

Introduction
   I Am but an Instrument...................................................................3
   Faithful Shepherd of Thy Flock ......................................................5
   True Seer of God.............................................................................6
   True Follower of Jesus ....................................................................8
   Override My Sin, Pardon the Frailty of Thy Servant.....................13
   The Main Thing ...........................................................................15
   Invitation to the Blessed Life.........................................................16

Life with God in Solitude
   "O Power of Love, All Else Transcending".................................21
   The Castle of My Soul..................................................................22
   Soon the Silvery Light Will Rest on It All ....................................23
   Haunted by Strange Shadows.......................................................24
   An Aid to Revelation....................................................................25
   All the Universe a Revelation of God ..........................................26
   Learn to Know God......................................................................27
   True Christianity...........................................................................28
   The Writings of John....................................................................29
   The Eternal Life ...........................................................................30
   Eternal Life Is New Life ................................................................31
   Knowledge and the Eternal Life ...................................................32
   Knowledge that Dominates Affections and Will...........................33
   Turning Knowledge to Conviction...............................................34
   The Measure of the Eternal Life in Us .........................................35
   We Small Creatures Know God?..................................................36

| | |
|---|---|
| The Only God Whom We Can Know | 37 |
| Knowing Christ Is Knowing God | 38 |
| Eternal Life Pouring into Our Hearts | 39 |
| This Is Indeed the Life Eternal | 40 |
| Learn from Madam Guyon | 41 |
| Embrace the Good Thing Despite the Excesses | 42 |
| Restless Souls | 43 |
| Heartbeats | 44 |
| Seek, Yield, Keep Open, Press Onward | 45 |
| Eternal Tendencies in the Human Soul | 46 |
| Not All of Christianity | 47 |
| It Is Possible | 48 |
| There Are Still Ardent Hearts | 49 |
| A Power Direct from the Unseen World | 50 |
| A Cry of Need | 51 |
| The Profoundest Classification of People | 52 |
| A Strange Sweetness | 53 |
| The Ifs of Prayer | 54 |
| A Breathing Space | 55 |
| Prayer and Morality | 56 |
| Emotionless Spirituality Is Valueless | 57 |
| Talk Out as You Feel | 58 |
| Re-establishing the Teachings of Jesus | 59 |
| The Final Word for Christian Minds | 60 |
| The Rarest Secret of All | 61 |
| Sharing the Secret | 62 |
| The Deceitfulness of Riches | 63 |
| Those Jesus Ridiculed | 64 |
| The Reign of Hate | 65 |
| What Hate Really Is | 66 |

The Real Thing ........................................................................................... 67
Keep Moving Forward ............................................................................. 68
Taught What to See ................................................................................. 69
Dear Mother…I Have to Believe What Is True ....................................... 70
Dear Mother…I Cannot Do Otherwise ................................................... 71
Dear Mother…I Am Stepping into Your Footsteps ................................ 72
Tell God Your Pains ................................................................................. 73
Present Illness and Final Requests ........................................................... 74
Life Is Still Worth Living .......................................................................... 76
Poems and Hymns for Life with God in Solitude .................................... 77
    Hymns of the Church ......................................................................... 77
    "Jerusalem, the Golden" ..................................................................... 78
    "The Sands of Time Are Sinking" ...................................................... 79
    "Thanksgiving" ................................................................................... 80
    "My Country" ..................................................................................... 81
    "Still, Still with Thee" ......................................................................... 82

Life with God in Service
    "Commit You All that Grieves You" .................................................. 84
    Inward and Outward .......................................................................... 85
    A New Feeling about Christ .............................................................. 86
    Urged to Give Up ............................................................................... 87
    For the Lord Christ and the People ................................................... 88
    Hold the Balance Even ....................................................................... 89
    The Heart of Jesus's Heart ................................................................. 90
    A Fulcrum for God's Lever ................................................................ 91
    Jesus Took Her Side ........................................................................... 92
    Not Aristocratic Charity ..................................................................... 93
    A New Avatar of Love ........................................................................ 94
    The Prophets ...................................................................................... 95
    Heartbeats become Pulse-Throbs ...................................................... 96

Copying a Prophet ............................................................................ 97

If the Prophets Lived Today ............................................................ 98

The Worship God Demands ............................................................ 99

The Mountain Was There .............................................................. 100

From Future Gaze to Here and Now Task ...................................... 101

The Kingdom Here and Now ......................................................... 102

To This Task We Dedicate Our Lives .............................................. 103

For the Gospel to Have Power Over an Age ................................... 104

Pulpit and Social Questions ........................................................... 105

Church and Politics ....................................................................... 106

Preachers, Pastors, and Prophets .................................................... 107

Flowerpot Religion ........................................................................ 108

Modern Christianity Is Not Christian Enough .............................. 109

Protector of the Vulnerable ............................................................ 110

Wealth Is Timid of Change ............................................................ 111

Christmas and the Cross ................................................................ 112

Christmas and Purposeful Suffering .............................................. 113

The Corruption of Christmas ........................................................ 114

A River Flowing from the Throne of God ..................................... 115

Divine Transformation of All Human Life .................................... 116

Character and Community Transformation .................................. 117

The Great Thing ............................................................................ 118

Has the Church Lost Its Saltiness? ................................................. 119

Teaching of the Church and the Ethics of Jesus ............................. 120

Has the Church Had Its Day? ........................................................ 121

The Most Searching Test of the Church ........................................ 122

Christianized Commerce or Commercialized Church? ................. 123

Make the Trial ............................................................................... 124

Blemishes of the Body of Christ .................................................... 125

The Church Has Not Kept Pace .................................................... 126

Church and Money Power .................................................................... 127
The American Church in the Hour of Trial ............................................ 128
The Church: Help or Hindrance? ........................................................... 129
The Spirit of Jesus .................................................................................. 130
God's Pioneers are Always Few .............................................................. 131
The Church Is Where the Spirit Is .......................................................... 132
The Most Daring Faith ........................................................................... 133
A New Apostolate in a New Harvest Time ............................................ 134
Before We Pass Away .............................................................................. 135
Poems and Hymns for Life with God in Service .................................... 136
    Hymns of Social Redemption ........................................................... 136
    "God Save America" ......................................................................... 137
    "Pikes Peak" ...................................................................................... 138
    "God of the Nations, Near and Far" ................................................ 139
    "When Wilt Thou Save the People?" ............................................... 140
    A Responsive Prayer for All Who Labor ......................................... 141
    "They Will Say" ................................................................................ 142
    A Psalm of Great Cities .................................................................... 143
    "O Love that Wilt Not Let Me Go" .................................................. 144

Life with God in Solidarity
"O God of Earth and Altar" ................................................................... 146
History and the Dominant Classes ......................................................... 147
Speaking with Symbols .......................................................................... 148
Speaking of Salvation ............................................................................. 149
Whenever Jesus Looked ......................................................................... 150
Does It Draw People Together? .............................................................. 151
God Looking at Us through the Eyes of Others .................................... 152
The Sociable Jesus .................................................................................. 153
Our Business ........................................................................................... 154
Love Creates Fellowship ......................................................................... 155

The Principle and Practice of Koinonia ........................................................ 156
Putting Our Feet Under the Same Table......................................................... 157
The Gregarious Nature of Humanity............................................................. 158
Bound Together in Unity of Life .................................................................. 159
The Goodness Jesus Seeks ........................................................................... 160
The Highest Type of Goodness..................................................................... 161
Systemic Affinity of Christianity .................................................................. 162
Justice ......................................................................................................... 163
The Power of Public Opinion....................................................................... 164
The Reign of Fear Is Never the Reign of God ............................................... 165
A Nation of Backsliders................................................................................ 166
When Nations Die....................................................................................... 167
The Abolition of Rank and Badges of Rank.................................................. 168
Unhorsing Privilege...................................................................................... 169
Private Interest and Chronic Corruption...................................................... 170
Class Chasm ................................................................................................ 171
Riches, Relations, and Renunciation ............................................................ 172
The Charm and Curse of Riches................................................................... 173
Economics and Politics ................................................................................ 174
An Outrageous Betrayal of Justice ................................................................ 175
A De Facto Emperor .................................................................................... 176
Forgive and Repair Torn Tissues................................................................... 177
The Real Zest of Life.................................................................................... 178
The Pronunciamento and Platform of Christianity....................................... 179
The Barrier Is Still Broad ............................................................................. 180
Open to All Who Will Come In .................................................................. 181
The Nerve of the Social Movement .............................................................. 182
Shoulder to Shoulder ................................................................................... 183
One Torch Kindling Hundreds .................................................................... 184
Let Us Counsel Patience............................................................................... 185

| | |
|---|---|
| The Process Is Never Complete | 186 |
| No Smooth Road | 187 |
| A Solidarity of Hate and Horror | 188 |
| Hate and War | 189 |
| A Prayer in Time of War, 1914 | 190 |
| Seek the Always-But-Coming Kingdom | 192 |
| Poems and Hymns for Life with God in Solidarity | 193 |
|     Woodrow Wilson's Prayer | 193 |
|     "The Preacher's Mistake" | 194 |
|     "For All the Saints" | 195 |
| Reflections on the Passion and Death of Jesus | |
| Jesus and the Social Movement | 197 |
| Capitalism and the Common Good | 198 |
| Jesus, the Solidarist | 199 |
| Let Jesus Speak | 200 |
| Go in the Direction of the Master | 201 |
| Law and Order | 202 |
| If, Then | 203 |
| What It Comes Down To | 204 |
| Economic Inequality and Political Equality | 205 |
| Yeasty with Privilege | 206 |
| Crossing Racial Boundary Lines, Outgrowing Nationalistic Religion | 207 |
| Not Only Mercy, but Justice | 208 |
| Dare We? | 209 |
| "Holy Fortitude" | 210 |
| Reflections on Thanksgiving | |
| "A Thanksgiving Meditation" | 212 |
| Quotation Sources | 216 |
| Primary Rauschenbusch Sources | 216 |
|     Books, Essay, Articles, Addresses | 216 |

Rauschenbusch Family Collection ........................................................... 217
Secondary Sources.................................................................................. 217
Reflection References.............................................................................. 218

# Foreword

My father was named after his famous grandfather and occasionally someone, often a pastor, would ask: "Any relation?" Aside from these episodes, our family awareness of Walter Rauschenbusch came through the recitation of his prayers. We would read them at family dinners, Thanksgiving, and other gatherings. Only much later, when I attended seminary myself, would I read my great-grandfather's books such as *Christianity and the Social Crisis*, or *A Theology for the Social Gospel* and appreciate the intellectual brilliance, linguistic dexterity and profound social commitment that he brought to his life as a seminary professor and pastor.

However, it is still the prayers and the spiritual writings that I heard as a child that continue to captivate me. Rauschenbusch is sometimes called a prophet, yet he might just as easily be deemed a mystic. Indeed, when Rauschenbusch is at his most powerful he is a combination of both mystic and prophet—both feeling the heart of God and demanding that God's love might be realized in justice "on earth as in heaven." My favorite Rauschenbusch writing starts with:

> "In the castle of my soul
> is a little postern gate,
> Whereat, when I enter,
> I am in the presence of God.
> In a moment, in the turning of a thought,
> I am where God is.
> This is a fact."

Here is the mystical presence with God that Walter invites us into, however it does not stop there as later in the reflection he writes:

> "So it is when my soul steps through the postern gate
> Into the presence of God.
> Big things become small, and small things become great.
> The near becomes far, and the future is near.
> The lowly and despised is shot through with glory,
> And most of human power and greatness
> Seems as full of internal iniquities
> As a carcass is full of maggots.
> God is the substance of all revolutions."

I am still moved by these words. How glorious to be invited into communion with God, as well as propelled into awareness of the world as seen through God's vision and inspired into action. Over the past century, many thousands have been moved in such a way by Rauschenbusch's words. The book you have in your hand, lovingly curated by Dennis L. Johnson, brings Rauschenbusch back in front of new readers and offers some of Walter Rauschenbusch's most mystical as well as prophetic writings to inspire us today. *Life with God* is an invitation to spirituality, yes, and oh, do we need spiritual sustenance for the living of these days. Yet it is also a hopeful offering, reminding us that our life with God offers retreat into our souls in order to be made stronger for our walk and our work for peace and justice for all.

My nine-year-old son is also named Walter, continuing the name in the family. He, and his brother Glenn are entering a world that has great promise yet is still rife with suffering and war. I'm grateful to Dennis for putting this book together, and my prayer is that you who are reading this book, along with me and so many others will be emboldened by a *Life with God* to create a world that reflects the heart of God, a world that Dr. King called "The Beloved Community"—a mystical and prophetic vision that Jesus offers us that continues to call out to us even today.

Paul Brandeis Raushenbush
Interfaith Alliance, President, CEO
2024

# Introduction

## I Am but an Instrument

As I grew up in our family Presbyterian church in rural Illinois, number 541 in the hymnbook was a thirteenth-century prayer/poem by Richard of Chichester (1197–1253) that we sang from time to time as a congregational choir:

> Day by day, Dear Lord, of Thee three things I pray:
> To see Thee more clearly, Love Thee more dearly,
> Follow Thee more nearly day by day.[1]

We were singing Bishop Richard's prayer long before the Broadway musical *Godspell* made it popular with "Day by Day" in the 1970s. Whether prayed 700 years ago or today, and whether sung or spoken in worship or in the solitude of one's devotion, it is a fine prayer. Many valuable spiritual guides from a wide range of Christian traditions and faith perspectives have mentored me into this ancient/contemporary prayer of a day-by-day spiritual life.

More than four decades ago, however, I—as a Baptist—wanted a Baptist among my guides for spiritual formation and pastoral ministry, and I found that Baptist guide in Walter Rauschenbusch (1861–1918). I have journeyed with him down a long stretch of road, and I still travel in his company as the road goes on. With his words and witness, his personal story and public writings, this Baptist pastor, seminary professor, and social prophet continues to help me as a Baptist see Christ more clearly, love Christ more dearly, and follow Christ more nearly, which is a day-by-day, ongoing, never-ceasing process.

Walter Rauschenbusch is a valuable formative guide not only for those within the Baptist tribe. He came from a long linage of German Lutherans, including seven generations of German Lutheran pastors. His father, a German Lutheran pastor, and mother abandoned the Lutheran tradition to become Baptists. Yet, while he was born into a Baptist family in Rochester, New York, Walter claimed his Baptist identity not simply by heritage but intentionally by conviction with breadth and expansiveness. Writing in 1905 about why he was a Baptist, he enlarged his identity by saying,

> Baptists are not a perfect denomination. We are capable of being just as narrow and small as anybody…. I do not want to foster Baptist self-conceit, because thereby I should grieve the Spirit of Christ. I do not want to

make Baptists shut themselves up in their little clamshells and be indifferent to the ocean outside of them. I am a Baptist, but I am more than a Baptist. All things are mine; whether Francis of Assisi, or Luther, or Knox, or Wesley; all things are mine because I am Christ's.[2]

This is one of the reasons Rauschenbusch has been such a valuable gift for my spiritual formation and for claiming an authentic Baptist identity. I haven't always been a Baptist. I come from a long line of Presbyterians. I graduated as a Presbyterian from a Franciscan university. I began study at a Baptist seminary as a Presbyterian and graduated from that seminary as a Baptist. But I experienced and still experience spiritual nurture from each of these streams of Christian tradition and from writers within each tradition. My heart warms when Rauschenbusch affirms that as a Baptist, he is not an isolationist, a separatist, a tribalist, a clamshell Baptist. He does not support a narrow, self-conceited spirituality. His is an "all-things-are-mine" spirituality because "I am Christ's." Rauschenbusch sees and loves and follows the All-who-is-in-all God; the all-inclusive Christ; the barrierless, borderless, boundless Spirit. He lives and moves and has his being in the Beginning and the End, the Divine Transcendence and Divine Immanence, the Poet of the Universe and the Source of all Splendor. To live and move otherwise is to grieve the Spirit of Christ. Rauschenbusch is a spiritual guide for more than Baptists because he is more than a Baptist. He is a spiritual mentor for all who are serious about following Jesus in Christlikeness day by day in their lifetimes.

Certainly, Walter Rauschenbusch is known as a groundbreaking theologian and justice-seeking social reformer, but in those roles he speaks with the voice of experience as a pastor. This has informed my essential perception of him and formed my deepest attachment to him. He has always been for me, first and foremost, Pastor Rauschenbusch.

He was a pastor. He fellowshipped with pastors. He read and studied and prayed with pastors when he was a pastor. He nurtured pastors. He identified with pastors. He knew from experience the sins and challenges and temptations of pastors. When he prayed for ministers, he included himself:

> O Jesus, we thy ministers bow before thee to confess the common sins of our calling. Thou knowest all things; thou knowest that we love thee and that our hearts' desire is to serve thee in faithfulness; and yet, like Peter, we have so often failed thee in the hour of thy need.... O Master, amidst our failures we cast ourselves upon thee in humility and contrition. We need new light and a new message. We need the ancient spirit of prophecy and the leaping fire and joy of a new conviction, and thou alone canst give it.... Free us from all entanglements that have hushed our voice and

bound our action…. Make us faithful shepherds of thy flock, true seers of God, and true followers of Jesus.³

As he prayed for all ministers to become and be, Pastor Rauschenbusch prayed for himself to become and be one of those "faithful shepherds of thy flock, true seers of God, and true followers of Jesus," and as a pastor he speaks to me. Now as then, he seeks for us, whether pastors or parishioners, within and beyond our particular spiritual tradition, to see Jesus more clearly, love him more dearly, and follow him more nearly day by day.

## Faithful Shepherd of Thy Flock

After he got a taste of pastoral ministry by serving a small German Baptist congregation in Louisville, Kentucky, for two summers during seminary, all Walter ever wanted to be was a pastor. In an 1884 letter to a seminary friend, he said, "It is now no longer my fond hope to be a learned theologian and write big books; I want to be a pastor…. And if I do ever become anything but a pastor, you may believe that I have sunk to a lower ideal or that there was a very unmistakable call to duty in that direction."⁴

That Louisville congregation was for him an eye-opening and heart-warming experience. He wrote to a friend that he found

> a small flock but a very neglected one. Sins of pastors and sins of members had created distrust and contempt among outsiders. Internal dissensions had banished the spirit of Brotherly Love. Everybody was sorely discouraged and very many were very hungry—which was the best thing about the church. I began with the determination to raise the spiritual standard of every Christian among them as far as he or she would let me. I worked a great deal from house to house, poopooed and frowned on their backbiting stories, reconciled those who hated each other and tried everywhere to awaken in their hearts the love of Christ as the only sure cure for their love of self and sin. Then I preached as well as I could and had the satisfaction of seeing the congregation almost double in 3 months. I organized the young people, gave Bible readings, in short I pitched in. As for the externals I lived on the hospitality of one family and got $20 a month; when I left the place I was as thin as a ghost, but I rejoiced in a number of conversions. I saw the members united by their common affection for their common Master, I saw them deeply affected when I said farewell when I left them…, and I was satisfied…. Again and again I said to myself, "How foolish I sh'd be, were I to attribute this to myself! This is beyond

my vainest imaginings about my powers; there is One behind me, I am but the instrument in his hand."[5]

That Louisville experience was enough to convince him to follow the call to be a pastor, and he would discover that being a pastor would call him to be an instrument and that being a pastor/instrument would call him to be a prophetic voice and agent of change as a servant of the Word.

## True Seer of God

The day came when, after spending two summers in Louisville and graduating from Rochester Theological Seminary at the age of twenty-five, Walter Rauschenbusch began his pastoral ministry amid the poverty and squalor, disease and crime of New York City's notorious Hell's Kitchen neighborhood. It wasn't long before he was obsessed with two issues: the spiritual care of his congregation and the social conditions of the city that separated the rich from the poor. With the convergence of these two issues, he was converted to the realization that the gospel of Jesus Christ is more than individual and about more than an afterlife. The young pastor came to save souls, and he realized there was more to be saved than souls. He encountered urban poverty and corruption; immigrant exploitation and unemployment; filth-plagued, stench-infested, oppressively overcrowded tenements; disease and death—so much death. He agonized over all the funerals he conducted, especially those of children. Throughout his Hell's Kitchen ministry, the young pastor was haunted by the question, "Why did the children have to die?"[6] These day-by-day realities in his ministry life were formative experiences that shaped him as a person, a pastor, a preacher, and a prophet in his time and as a guide for later generations of Jesus-followers.

In the winter of 1888, a year into his ministry, even more suffering came to pass with an influenza epidemic. Many of the poor froze to death on the streets of New York City. The young pastor so exhausted himself tending to his duties and caring for his people that he too became ill and was confined to bed. When he received word of a parishioner in need, he rose from his bed, still sick and weak, to go to his friend. As a result of leaving his sickbed too soon, his hearing was affected and he sensed it beginning to fade. It was not long before the gift of hearing was gone. He sought medical attention, but nothing could be done to restore his hearing, and he was forced to live with what he described as a "physical loneliness." At age twenty-seven, he entered a world of silence, only to be left with a surf-like roar that never ceased day by day, night by night, for the rest of his life. When he died, his wife Pauline, whom he married in 1893 and whose voice he never heard clearly, wrote to their son Hilmar in France that at last his father was free—"free from care and worry and sickness and can hear. Think of it, he can hear, Hilmar."[7] As a shepherd of Christ's flock and as a true seer of God, the good pastor sacrificed his health for the love of his people.

Pastor Rauschenbusch decided in 1891 that the hearing loss left him inadequate to fulfill his calling and that he was no longer able to carry out his pastoral duties. So, with deep sadness, he resigned as pastor of Second German Baptist. Rochester Seminary had offered him a faculty position, but he turned it down, believing being a deaf professor was as unrealistic as being a deaf pastor. The church, however, refused his resignation and asked him to take a year's sabbatical, then return as their pastor. With the church's love and grace, he remained with them for six more years, during which he married and started a family.

His pastoral vocation in Hell's Kitchen was the anvil on which he forged his spirituality, his calling, his theology, his social vision of the gospel, and his kingdom vision of life as it ought to be. It formed within him the insistence that the will and realm of God must prevail in the totality of one's being and in every aspect of human existence; that salvation is a transformation from self-centeredness and self-interest to an orientation toward God and others and the common good. Life and ministry during those eleven Hell's Kitchen years opened the eyes of Walter's heart to see Jesus more clearly and love him more dearly and follow him more nearly day by day. And he was not alone.

During those years, he formed a fellowship with two other like-minded neighboring pastors. They met weekly for Bible study, devotional reading, theological reflection, worship, the Lord's Supper, and envisioning ways to apply the social ethics of Jesus in the community. On July 9, 1892, in Rauschenbusch's New York City apartment, the fellowship of three expanded to a group of six and launched the "Brotherhood of the Kingdom," which grew in membership from a variety of Protestant traditions, included women, and became an international fellowship. For the next thirty years, the Brotherhood met annually in Marlborough, New York, with members presenting papers, speeches, and debates exploring together the practical application of the ethics of Jesus and the reign of God in human society.

After eleven years as pastor of the Second German Baptist Church of New York City, Walter accepted in 1897 Rochester Seminary's second invitation to join the faculty. His final Sunday as pastor was July 4, 1897. In his farewell sermon that Sunday evening, the last words his beloved flock heard from their faithful shepherd and true seer of God were these two final sentences: "If it is painful to part, remember that it was good to be together. And this shall be my joy and crown, if I hear and see you pressing onward in the footsteps of Jesus Christ to whom I have tried to lead you."[8] Those parting words reflect the heart of Walter Rauschenbusch, and they remain his good words to our generation and every generation—press onward in the footsteps of Jesus Christ. To see others of every generation pressing onward in the footsteps of Jesus remains his crown and joy.

He carried that pastoral passion with him when his ministry setting changed from the local church in New York City to a seminary community in upstate New York. In the academia of Rochester Theological Seminary, he shaped seminarians preparing to be pastors, retained a pastor's heart, and remained a minister of Jesus to students and faculty in the seminary community and the community of Rochester and beyond. He continued to be a faithful shepherd of Christ's flock, a true seer of God, and a true follower of Jesus.

## True Follower of Jesus

As a drama student in college, I learned that the way to get to know the character of a person in a play is by what the person says, what others say to the person, and what others say about the person. We know what Walter Rauschenbusch said in his books, lectures, correspondence, articles, essays, sermons, and speeches, and to know him better we can turn with trust to those who knew him and spoke with him and hear what they have said about him. They help us know his being and character. Among them are his seminary colleagues and students. Thankfully we have a record of what some of them said about him on the sad occasion of his death.[9]

Following his death on July 25, 1918, family and friends gathered at the Rauschenbusch home in Rochester for his funeral on July 27, and the seminary community gathered for a memorial service that fall on November 18. We get a sense of the person and spirituality of Walter Rauschenbusch from the colleagues and students who knew him, learned from him, loved him, and served alongside him. From their experience, they give us a glimpse into Walter Rauschenbusch, the person and personality, the professor and prophet, the pastor of Christ's flock and preacher of Christ's gospel.

At the funeral service, seminary president Clarence Barbour said that his friend loved the church: "Among all other human institutions, he held her incomparable. He saw her by the eye of faith reborn for her great new task amid the perplexities of a changing order." He loved the people: "Especially the people who bore the burden and heat of the day." He loved the kingdom of God: "As a prophet of social righteousness he stood in the very front rank of the men of our day.... His books will continue in their work of ministry long after this day when the voice of their author is still." He loved Christ: "Christ was ever for him the living Christ."[10]

During the seminary memorial service, faculty, along with former students, shared words of insight and gratitude. Henry B. Robins, a Rochester Seminary professor and former student of Rauschenbusch, paid tribute, saying,

> It was borne in upon us that life is all of a piece.... The greatest contribution which Professor Rauschenbusch made to his students lay...in the religious spirit of the man himself.... There was a rare simplicity about his personal approach to God and a passionate yearning for genuine kinship of spirit and experience with Jesus Christ which suffused his whole bearing with an unfailing quality of reverence.... [He was,] in the best sense of the term, a Christian mystic. He believed in the continuity of inspiration and of the prophetic office.... He was a voice, not an echo.

Walter's most impactful lessons as a teacher to his students, Robins said, were that

> the past is no pattern, yet the clue to life is there. If we find that clue, we shall learn not to repeat yesterday's mistakes, yet at the same time we shall truly build upon the foundation which the ancestors laid. We shall approach the past with true reverence and humility, for God spoke there betimes and wrought there; but we shall not stand on naked fear of the past nor bound by all its trammels, for God speaks now and God is at work here in this our present order of life. How to be reverent and yet fearless, how to learn with meekness and at length to speak with authority—these were great lessons!
>
> And now he is gone from us. But ever and again that kindly face will illumine the chambers of our souls and the spirit of the man will speak to us. Those keen eyes will penetrate our inner selves, rebuking us always if we are not more truly our Master's disciples.[11]

Charles Osborn remembered as a student that "we found him to be a true friend." Rauschenbusch had the custom of taking students home with him for the noonday meal, "giving us an opportunity for close fellowship to his study and about the family table. We were made to feel at home in his presence."[12] He took personal interest in each student, especially their spiritual and social upbringing and the influences moving them to enter the ministry. Osborn added that in the classroom behind his lessons

> was a simple but fervent prayer that God would lay His Spirit upon us and inspire us with a passion of Christlike love, that we might join our lives to the weak and the oppressed and might have a part in strengthening their cause by bearing a portion of the burdens.
>
> The atmosphere of spiritual influence that he carried with him we realized was the outgrowth of a life that was spent in the closest and deepest fellowship with Jesus Christ. Because of his affliction we thought

him as living in a world of deep thought and meditation concerning those things which are nearest to the heart of God and most needful to man. To us he was one who possessed his soul in quietness and looked for the kingdom of peace.[13]

Former faculty colleague Cornelius Woelfkin, then senior minister of Fifth Avenue Baptist Church in New York City, said in his words of affirmation, "His own work will take its place in the perspective of the past, but the notes which he set vibrating will always sound.... He is dead yet speaketh."[14]

Edwin T. Dalhberg, student assistant of Rauschenbusch in 1917, told the gathered community,

> The winter when I was typing his correspondence for him, I saw more of his great heart revealed than I ever thought could be in any one. It will abuse no confidence if I tell you of the many cheerful letters he wrote to people all over the world, children in hospitals, Sunday School teachers out in Montana, men tired and worn out in their work, telling them about everything from little dogs to the kingdom of God. The silent influence of his letters upon my own life was something for which I shall always be grateful.[15]

Dahlberg became a leading and esteemed American Baptist pastor, theologian, and voice for peace and justice. He continued over the years to be a reliable commentator about Rauschenbusch. During an interview in which he shared his memories of his former professor, mentor, and friend, he told a story reflecting the caring pastoral heart of Rauschenbusch for everyone he encountered in life. At one point, the Rauschenbusch home was burglarized by a thief who stole a set of their china plates. The thief was caught, and Rauschenbusch was asked to come to the police station to retrieve the stolen items and press charges. Upon arriving, he saw the disheveled robber in ragged clothes. He made a surprising request and asked the police to release the man into his personal custody, which was arranged. The following weeks and months gave the faithful shepherd, true seer of God, and true follower of Jesus time to befriend the man and help him get a fresh start in life. The man was invited to dinner at the Rauschenbusch home one evening, and dinner was served on the very plates he had stolen. Years later, when Dahlberg was his student secretary, Rauschenbusch invited the man to class. The former thief shared his testimony with the students on how he came to Christ through the caring ministry of Walter Rauschenbusch.

There was another occasion, Dahlberg recalled, when Rauschenbusch paid the expenses for someone else, an ex-safecracker named Spike, to travel to Rochester and tell the students about his conversion experience. He had been on his way to rob a bank when he stopped by a Billy Sunday rally and experienced a new beginning.[16]

While those who spoke at the funeral and memorial services had unique impressions to share, one mutual, lasting memory and influence on them by their friend and teacher were the prayers of Walter Rauschenbusch. Rev. Woelfkin shared, "To hear him pray was to feel a benediction. He was like a child at his father's knee, speaking with simplicity, confidence and hope his requests of God."[17] "When Professor Rauschenbusch used to come out from behind his desk and pray at the beginning of each class," Edwin Dahlberg said, "we were all of us led so near to Christ that we shall always be better men for it." Professor Robins confessed that hearing Rauschenbusch pray made him "reflect upon the poverty of my own spiritual life whose poor expression was so in contrast with the wealth of his own.... These unforgettable prayers revealed the heart of our friend; they uncovered his imperishable treasure." Dean Joseph Stewart brought to mind a visit Rauschenbusch made to the seminary while he was still a pastor in New York City, and during their conversation the pastor spoke of "the privilege of prayer":

> I remember how he said that he invariably found rest and refreshing in prayer; that it not only revived his spirit, but also seemed to bring reversal of all his powers. Whatever his views of the Bible and of theology, he certainly led a most devout life. He "walked with God." He sought to bring his daily life, the inward life as well as the outward, constantly under the eye of God, our heavenly Father. None of us in this seminary will forget his prayers in our chapel. You could call on him to pray at any time and invariably you felt that his prayer was a real speaking to God. How simple, how beautiful, how direct, how heartfelt his prayers were![18]

The prayers in this collection of daily reflections include some of those simple, beautiful, direct, and heartfelt chapel prayers of Walter Rauschenbusch that have never been published.

While she was not among the speakers at his funeral or memorial services, Helen Barrett Montgomery, also a resident of Rochester, was a friend of Rauschenbusch and held him in high regard. She also was deeply touched by his prayers. In a letter to him after he gifted Helen and her husband William with a copy of *Prayers of the Social Awakening*, she wrote, "Will was not well yesterday, did not leave his room, and in the afternoon we had a very orgy of prayers—reading the entire book through. It was a strange way to read such a book—and I think it means much that we finished eager for more.... Thank you for the prayers every one. We are using the morning and evening and thanksgiving ones at family worship." She said that she particularly liked his "Prayers of Wrath," including those against war and serving mammon. She could enter them, she said, "and feel fierce and religious at the same time."[19] When I am asked by someone who is unfamiliar with Rauschenbusch what I suggest as the place to start reading, I always say, "If you want to know the heart of Walter Rauschenbusch, read his prayers. Begin with his prayers."

The Rochester Seminary memorial service closed with a prayer by Professor Albert Ramaker in which he asked for divine grace "that we may not forget that our beloved teacher, our brother and our friend, is still with us, though absent from the body. May we still listen to his helpful and inspiring counsel! May we feel the earnestness and devotion of his loving personality."[20]

Walter's years as a pastor-professor in the Rochester community and at Rochester Seminary furnished a full chapter in the story of his life, but it was not a long chapter, and it ended sadly for him. Referring to World War I, he wrote in his final plans in the event of his death, "Since 1914 the world is full of hate, and I can not expect to be happy again in my lifetime."[21] He was bitterly opposed to militarism and called for Americans to remain neutral in the conflict. He resisted demonizing Germany, the land of his ancestors and where his father and mother were buried.

His resistance to the war made him the target of intense criticism at a time of national patriotic fervor and hostility toward Germany. Friends and admirers turned against him. Unsigned letters with threats to him and his family began arriving at his home. The Rauschenbusch summer lakefront home in Canada was vandalized and burned to the ground. He was accused of loyalty to Germany over loyalty to America, of which he was a native-born citizen. German Americans came under heightened suspicion, and anti-German hostility grew in American public opinion. Seminary president Barbour announced in May 1917 that the seminary supported the war effort and gave assurance of the school's "absolute loyalty" to the nation. That was a stand Rauschenbusch had not taken.[22] Barbour and former faculty colleague Woelfkin apparently were concerned about the good name of their friend and his personal safety. They pushed him to reexamine his position about the war and encouraged him to make a public statement supporting the allied war effort. Compounding the physical suffering he experienced at the time due to, as of then, an unidentified cause was the painful, agonizing, and heartbreaking thought that his two friends joined forces against him and questioned his Christian convictions, loyalty, and patriotism. Nevertheless, in the summer of 1918, Rauschenbusch issued a public letter affirming the strength of America's democracy and condemning Germany's aggressive militarism; but he remained consistent with his essential convictions on war and peace and the loss of love. The letter was met with relief by some and disappointment by others who saw it as a tragic mistake. His daughter Winifred called it "the one great mistake" of his life. It was, she said, "a little lack of courage in a man who otherwise had great courage."[23] In a matter of weeks, he was dead, his writing coming true: "I can not expect to be happy again in my lifetime."

Walter's thoughts on war and the loss of love, and his 1914 prayer in a time of war, are included in this collection of daily reflections. To his end, he remained "with staff in hand…in quest of the Holy Grail of truth."[24] His Christian faith and formation was a process of being grounded in prayer and spiritual discernment and being shaped by the Word. His being and doing were centered in Christlikeness and committed to applying the teachings of Jesus to contemporary life and society in the direction of equality, community, freedom, love, justice, and solidarity. Christ-confession, for Rauschenbusch, was authentic only with Christ-following. Personal salvation and social salvation were never to be divorced. His deep personal spirituality moved him into social confrontation and transformation with the Spirit of Jesus. Faith in Jesus demands following the teachings of Jesus, not just admiring Jesus and his teachings. Jesus is looking for disciples, students, followers—not fans. Rauschenbusch sought to be as best he could a follower of Jesus, and he challenged churches to form Christian Christians who dared to follow the footprints of Jesus rather than be admirers of Jesus. His spirituality was evangelical, compassionate, inclusive, and caring enough to confront the kingdom of evil with the kingdom of God.

More than a century after his death, Walter Rauschenbusch is still able to lead us to Jesus and help us see Jesus more clearly, love him more dearly, and follow him—press onward in his footsteps—more nearly day by day on a journey of inner quiet with social action in human solidarity.

## Override My Sin, Pardon the Frailty of Thy Servant

My attachment to Walter Rauschenbusch as a spiritual guide willingly acknowledges his feet of clay and his falling short of fully incarnating the Jesus principle of love and solidarity he embraced and taught. He has inconsistencies and paradoxes and problems. There is no denying or turning a blind eye to his blind spots. Then again, blind spots and deficiencies are ripe for criticism and easy to spot 100 years later—just as our generation's blind spots will be pointed out 100 years from now. That thought alone should help us look back with humility on all the saints who now rest from their labors. As historian of American religion Margaret Bendroth reminds us, "Discovering that great saints failed to avoid the pitfalls of their time may make us cynical, but it can also make us wiser about our common human condition. All told, they are no worse and no better than us…. Historical perspective should make us more humble and cautious about ourselves. People from the past were not the only ones operating with a cultural context—we have one, too."[25]

The deficiencies in Rauschenbusch's thought and comments should not be glossed over today. He is a product of his time and reflects his moment in history. He emulates the cultural context and worldview of the late nineteenth-century Victorian era with its American Protestant Christianity, characterized by white, paternalistic, middle-upper class domination. As he lived and ministered among the suffering and exploited immigrant working poor in urban New York City, he grappled with and responded to the economic and social injustices of industrialism as well as the unchecked business practices and unregulated capitalism of the Gilded Age. He brought that experience and his convictions with him when upstate New York became his ministry setting as a seminary professor and the place where he wrote his bestselling books, *Christianity and the Social Crisis* (1907) and *Christianizing the Social Order* (1912). He was planted in particular social locations at a particular moment in history, which was where and when he sought, with feet of clay, to press onward in the footsteps of Jesus.[26]

Yet, in his particular time and space, within his cultural context and ministry settings, and with his failures to avoid pitfalls of his time, Walter Rauschenbusch points us to what is essential in his and in our mutual Christian faith. With wisdom and weaknesses, holy vision and blind spots, Rauschenbusch captured the imagination of his generation and the passion of ensuing generations by his insistence that we cannot claim to be followers of Jesus if we do not reflect the image of Jesus, the spirit of Jesus, and the ethics of Jesus. We cannot follow Jesus unless, in the words of Henri Nouwen, we serve in memory of Jesus as living reminders of Jesus.[27] The pursuit for truth and the gospel demand for love, justice, and solidarity must persist in each generation's moment and social location in history. Each generation must confront injustices of their own time as Rauschenbusch tried to do in his own time. During his lifetime, Rauschenbusch prepared the soil and planted seeds that grew into contemporary expressions of living out the gospel of Jesus Christ as mandates and manifestations of a kingdom "that is always but coming."[28] As Cornelius Woelfkin affirmed in his tribute to Rauschenbusch, "the notes which he set vibrating will always sound. He is dead, yet he speaks."

I often wonder how his mind would have changed had he not died so young. Would his thoughts have expanded, his words been different, his works been more consistent with his words, and his voice been given sooner to the evil of racism, about which he had been silent for so long? He was still forming and still a quester for truth to the very end. Where would his mind have gone, and where would his voice have been heard, if he were blessed with twenty more years for reflection, discernment, proclamation, writing, and action? As he anticipated his death, he included in his final plans, "For my errors and weaknesses, I hope to be forgiven by my fellows." Embracing his errors and weaknesses, his bundle of paradoxes and blind spots and sin, has freed me to read Rauschenbusch beyond Rauschenbusch. It has enabled me to look upon him and myself and all of us as sharing a common human condition. Each of us have feet of clay, and none of us avoid the pitfalls of our time. As historian Bendroth counsels us, we should not forget the certainty that our own descendants will shake their heads in disbelief about the impossible things we took for granted and the evils we accepted without protest.[29]

The final prayer Rauschenbusch offers in his 1910 *Prayers of the Social Awakening* is a prayer for himself. In it I hear his never-ending willingness and heartfelt openness to confront his deficiencies and weaknesses, his shortcomings and sin, his frailty and faults. I hear his desire for a change of heart and a mind more conformed to the image and likeness of Jesus. He prayed,

> O thou who art the light of my soul, I thank thee for the incomparable joy of listening to thy voice within, and I know that no word of thine shall return void, however brokenly uttered. If aught in this book was said through lack of knowledge, or through weakness of faith in thee or of love for others, I pray thee to overrule my sin and turn aside its force before it harm thy cause. Pardon the frailty of thy servant, and look upon him only as he sinks his life in Jesus, his Master and Savior. Amen.

His own prayerful words provide a way for us to look upon Walter Rauschenbusch, which is the way he prayed for his Creator to look upon him—"only as he sinks his life in Jesus, his Master and Savior." I have found that this is a good and gracious, honest and humble way to look upon one who sought to immerse his life in Jesus more deeply and follow the holy ways of Jesus more fully each day.

## The Main Thing

After moving from his life as a pastor in New York City to his position as a seminary professor in Rochester, Rauschenbusch was asked that first year (1897) to deliver the commencement address to the graduating students in the German department. Of all the important and pressing matters that this first-year faculty member—an experienced and beloved pastor, social gospeler, and soon-to-be trailblazing theologian—could address, what was his subject? The title of his message was "The Culture of the Spiritual Life." His comments received a wider audience once the message was published in the November 1897 edition of *The Rochester Baptist Monthly*. In his closing words, Walter gives his vision of the spiritual life, the life with God, the life he calls blessed:

> But the main thing is to have God; to live in Him; to have Him live in us; to think His thoughts; to love what He loves and hate what He hates;

to realize His presence; to feel His holiness and to be holy because He is holy; to feel His goodness in every blessing of our life and even in its tribulations; to be happy and trustful; to join the great purposes of God and to be lifted to greatness of vision and faith and hope with Him—that is the blessed life.[30]

With less than one hundred words, Rauschenbusch paints in broad strokes life with God as the blessed life, and more than a century later he continues to challenge us to cultivate, nurture, and grow in our life with God more fully, more freely, and more fearlessly, pressing onward in the footsteps of Jesus.

The more I have walked with Rauschenbusch over the years, the more I have been drawn to his depiction of this "main thing," this "blessed life," this life with God in the spirit of Jesus. I am convinced this life is *the* life to be lived. Scottish professor John Baillie put it well: "What makes one a Christian is neither one's intellectual acceptance of certain ideas nor one's conformity to a certain rule, but one's possession of a certain Spirit and participation in a certain life."[31] That "certain spirit" is the Christ-Spirit. That "certain life" is the Christlike life. My conviction is that this life with God is the life to be lived day by day for meaningful, purposeful human existence, for spiritual vitality and congregational vibrancy, and for social transformation. It is the life a follower of Jesus is to incarnate in memory of Jesus and a church is to embody as the Body of the living Christ. Life with God is "the main thing." When we feel spiritually bankrupt, this life beckons us to newness in which there is thriving and well-being and delight. This life calls a dry, declining, dying congregation to catch the wind of the Spirit so they may flourish and be refreshed and animated in the kingdom of God. This life is the blessed way for being human with one another in the world. It is the main thing for followers of Jesus and the Body of Christ. My conviction is that God summons us in Jesus Christ through the power of the Spirit to embrace and embody life with God for as long as we live in this old world God loves so much.

## Invitation to the Blessed Life

Over the years I have pondered the writings and life of Walter Rauschenbusch with particular focus on his spirituality. I have discerned in him an inward, outward, and common journey that I used in *To Live in God* to format six months of daily Rauschenbusch reflections.[32] These are not three separate journeys but a single journey with multiple dimensions of loving God and the people we encounter in life. I offer this second book with more daily reflections from Rauschenbusch as an invitation to explore with him the life with God he calls "blessed." This present collection continues a threefold pattern: Life with God in Solitude, Life with God in Service, and Life with God in Solidarity.

*To Live in God* drew primarily from Walter's major books, *Christianity and the Social Crisis, Christianizing the Social Order,* and *A Theology for the Social Gospel,* as well as his lesser-known books, *Come Unto Me, Dare We be Christians?* and *The Social Principles of Jesus.* While this second collection also draws from some of those works, many reflections are culled from his essays and articles, his favorite hymns and poems, his personal scrapbooks and poetry notebooks, and his unpublished manuscripts, sermons, and prayers.[33]

Each reflection opens with a passage of scripture on which to meditate as preparation for the Rauschenbusch passage. The brief New Testament excerpts from these passages are translated by Baptist contemporaries of Rauschenbusch: Helen Barrett Montgomery and Edgar Goodspeed. Each daily reflection concludes with lines from prayers preserved in the Rauschenbusch Family Collection at the American Baptist Historical Society. Minor modifications to the historic texts of Rauschenbusch, Montgomery, and Goodspeed have been made to minimize masculine God language and to use gender-inclusive language for human beings. I have also adapted the prayers from his traditional "thee" and "thine" to "you" and "your."

I have formatted each reflection and prayer in a way that exhibits the poetic character of Rauschenbusch's prose and also breaks up the sentences into shorter lines more compatible to reflective reading. I encourage you to read slowly, prayerfully, and contemplatively the full scripture passage, not just the quoted verse/verses, and the Rauschenbusch reflection and prayer. Perhaps journal your thoughts and ponderings as you ask yourself these questions:

- How am I being challenged to grow?
- How is God speaking to me?
- What is the Spirit asking me to be or do?
- What rough edges about me need smoothing into Christlikeness? Where or in what way am I being moved to sink my life in Jesus? Where am I being invited to press onward in the footsteps of Jesus?
- Of what do I need to let go so I will see Jesus more clearly, love him more dearly, and follow him more nearly as my dear Lord?

A blessed life with God is not about health and wealth, prosperity and privilege, getting rich and being popular. It is not a care-free or pain-free life. It is not an American life or a smooth path. A blessed life with God is a holy life, a challenging life, a wonderful life, a fulfilling life. It is life with One whose yoke is easy and whose burden is light (see Matt 11:30). It is wide and deep and soaring, encompassing the whole of life in which there is fullness and thriving and joy, joy, joy. It is a pilgrim life. It is life on the road. It is life together. We need each other. We travel together as companions, side by side, day by day. And one of our companions on the road is brother Walter.

The spirituality of Walter Rauschenbusch as a faithful shepherd of Christ's flock, a true seer of God, and a true follower of Jesus embraces a contemplative life of solitude, a compassionate life of service, and a communitarian life of solidarity with the world as a divine commonwealth. His story and service, his words and witness are still with us. He is still trying to lead us to Jesus Christ; still inspiring, guiding, provoking, wooing us to press onward in the footsteps of Jesus; still beckoning us to sink our life in Jesus with him. As his faculty colleague said during the seminary memorial service, "…the notes which he set vibrating will always sound…. He is dead, yet speaketh."[34]

Legend has it that Bishop Richard of Chichester offered his "day by day" prayer on his deathbed. Before he prayed his three memorable petitions, he opened his prayer with thanksgiving to his "most merciful Redeemer, friend and brother."

> Thanks be to Thee, my Lord Jesus Christ,
> For all the benefits thou hast given me,
> For all the pains and insults
> Thou hast borne for me.[35]

Whether or not he prayed the prayer from his deathbed, Bishop Richard died at age fifty-six. Six hundred sixty-five years later in 1918, Walter Rauschenbusch would die of cancer at age fifty-six.

He too knew with a thankful heart the benefits his most merciful redeemer, friend, and brother had given him in life. He knew the grace he had been granted amid pains and insults with which he bore "the marks of the Lord Jesus" and that Jesus bore with him. Walter Rauschenbusch sought to sink himself and his life into Jesus. He has guided generations of Christians into sinking and soaking our being, our doing, our lives in Jesus, whom we pray to see more clearly, love more dearly, and follow more nearly, day by day. This day-by-day life with God in solitude, service, and solidarity, is, as Paul wrote to young Timothy, "the Life which is life indeed" (1 Timothy 6:19, Montgomery).

## NOTES

[1]Richard of Chichester, "Day by Day, Dear Lord," *The Hymnbook* (Presbyterian Church in the United States, 1955), 541.

[2]Rauschenbusch, "Why I Am a Baptist," *The Baptist Leader* (January 1958): 7–17; originally published in *The Rochester Monthly* (November 1905; January, February, March 1906).

[3]Rauschenbusch, "Prayer for Ministers," *Prayers of the Social Awakening* (Boston: Pilgrim Press, 1910).

[4]Winthrop S. Hudson, ed., *Walter Rauschenbusch: Selected Writings* (Paulist Press, 1984), 53.

[5]Hudson, 53.

[6] Christopher H. Evans, *The Kingdom Always but Coming: A Life of Walter Rauschenbusch* (Grand Rapids, MI: Eerdmans, 2004), 62.

[7] Paul M. Minus, *Walter Rauschenbusch: American Reformer* (New York: Macmillan Publishing, 1988), 194. Letter written July 27, 1918.

[8] "Farewell Sermon," ABHS Rauschenbusch Family Collection, Box 139, vol. 39, pp. 140–155.

[9] Rochester Theological Seminary Bulletin [hereafter RTSB], "The Record," November 1918, 7, 8.

[10] RTSB, 7, 8.

[11] RTSB, 34, 35, 36.

[12] RTSB, 27, 28.

[13] RTSB, 28.

[14] RTSB, 23.

[15] RTSB, 77.

[16] John Skoglund, "Edwin Dahlberg in Conversation: Memories of Walter Rauschenbusch," *Foundations* 18, no. 3 (July–September 1975): 209–218. This is a journal publication by the American Baptist Historical Society.

[17] RTSB, 22.

[18] RTSB 25.

[19] Helen B. Montgomery to Walter Rauschenbusch, December 13, 1910, ABHS RFC, Box 17, Folder 7.

[20] RTSB, 36.

[21] Rauschenbusch, March 31, 1918, ABHS RFC 62-F7, Box 120, Folder 3.

[22] Minus, *Walter Rauschenbusch*, 183.

[23] Evans, *The Kingdom Always but Coming*, 308.

[24] Rauschenbusch, *Christianizing the Social Order* (New York: Macmillan Co, 1912), 10.

[25] Margaret Bendroth, *The Spiritual Practice of Remembering* (Grand Rapids, MI: Eerdmans, 2013), 49.

[26] Christian ethicist David Gushee has provided significant, comprehensive attention to the blind spots and paradoxes of Rauschenbusch and acknowledges the need to read Rauschenbusch beyond Rauschenbusch. For those wanting to explore more deeply the paradoxes and legacy of Rauschenbusch, Gushee's in-depth and extended introduction is a good place to begin. See "An Introduction to the Ethics of Walter Rauschenbusch," *Walter Rauschenbusch: Published Works and Selected Writings*, vol. 2, gen. ed. William Brackney (Macon, GA: Mercer University Press, 2018), vii-lxxviii.

[27] Henri J. M. Nouwen, *The Living Reminder: Service and Prayer in Memory of Jesus Christ* (Seabury Press, 1977).

[28] Rauschenbusch, *Christianity and the Social Crisis* (New York: Association Press, 1907), 421.

[29] Bendroth, *Spiritual Practice of Remembering*, 49.

[30] "The Culture of the Spiritual Life," *Rochester Baptist Monthly*, November 1897. In ABHS RFC, Box 63, File 2.

[31] John Baillie, *The Roots of Religion in the Human Soul* (London: Hodder & Stoughton, 1926), 203.

[32] Dennis L. Johnson, *To Live in God: Daily Reflections with Walter Rauschenbusch* (Valley Forge, PA: Judson Press, 2020).

[33] Many of these are from the Walter Rauschenbusch Family Collection archived at the American Baptist Historical Society in Atlanta. The entire collection contains 107 linear feet of files.

[34] RTSB, 23.

[35] "Prayer of Saint Richard of Chichester," *Loyola Press*, https://www.loyolapress.com/catholic-resources/prayer/traditional-catholic-prayers/saints-prayers/day-by-day-prayer-of-saint-richard-of-chichester/.

# Life with God in Solitude

# "O Power of Love, All Else Transcending"
## Gerhard Tersteegen (1697–1769)

*"Tersteegen was a friend of my grandparents. This hymn has often expressed the intimate feeling of my heart for Jesus, whose saving love has been everything to me."*
—On one of the hymns the dying Rauschenbusch requested, "on an occasion when convenient, I should like to have sung for me"

O power of love, all else transcending,
In Jesus present evermore,
We worship Thee, in homage bending,
And all Thy wondrous might adore.
Yea, let my soul, in deep devotion,
Bathe in love's mighty, boundless ocean.

Thou art my rest, no earthly treasure
Can satisfy my yearning heart,
And naught can give to me the pleasure
I find in Thee, my chosen part.
Thy love, so tender and caressing
Is joy to me and every blessing.

To Thee my heart and life be given,
Thou art in truth my highest Good;
For me Thy sacred side was riven,
For me was shed Thy precious blood.
O Thou who art the world's salvation,
Be Thine my love and adoration.

Gerhard Tersteegen, "O Power of Love," trans. Herman Breuckner, 1918, *Hymnary.org*, https://hymnary.org/text/o_power_of_love_all_else_transcending.

# The Castle of My Soul
## Psalm 23

*He restores my soul.*

Far away, on a wind-swept height, my soul has built her a castle,
  whither she retreats from the strife of men,
  and when the great gate swings to its lock,
    my soul is well content with its company.
For in the painted hall, under the groined arches,
  she has supped with great men.
    Isaiah has chanted to her in Hebrew, and Plato has discoursed in Attic,
    and many an historian has lifted the fringe of the Curtain of Seemly Lies
      that wraps the Book of Reality....
High above the castle, stretching into the starry infinity,
  is the watch tower of my soul.
    Thence she looks down on the kingdoms of this world
      and wants not their glory;
    and forward to the Things that Shall Be;
    and up to the sickle of Venus, and the rings of Saturn,
    and the belt of Orion, and the glorious locks of Cassiopeia,
    and my soul leaps to the Milky Way, bounding from star to star,
      where God strode down through Eternity
      when the morning stars sang to Him in the Youth of the World.
But beneath the castle is a dark corridor,
  which my soul would fain forget and cannot.
    However softly she steals past,
      ghosts creep forth, crying softly,
      and bidding her remember how she trampled on trust and love
        in blind ignorance or blinder anger,
    and she remembers.
This is the castle of my soul, and when my soul has locked the gate,
  her nearest kin lives 10,000 leagues away.

—May 1918

# Soon the Silvery Light Will Rest on It All

## 2 Corinthians 4:5-6

*For God who said, "Out of darkness light shall shine,"*
*Is the one who has shown in my heart, that the sunrise of the knowledge of God*
*may shine forth in the face of Christ.*
(verse 6, Montgomery)

The main thing is
   to have God;
   to live in God;
   to have God live in us;
   to think God's thoughts;
   to love what God loves and hate what God hates;
   to realize God's presence;
   to feel God's holiness and to be holy
     because God is holy;
   to feel God's goodness in every blessing of our life
     and even in its tribulations;
   to be happy and trustful;
   to join in the great purposes of God
     and to be lifted to greatness of vision and faith
        and hope with God—
that is the blessed life.
Let us not grieve if it is faint in us as yet.
   When a young moon is filling its slender crescent,
     the astronomer can watch little points and rings of light
        on the surface that is still dark.
The sunrise has struck the mountain tops of the moon.
   Those points and rings will widen
     and soon the silvery light will rest on it all.

*O God, as our hunger for joy and beauty and companionship and truth*
*expanded with our ripening years,*
*the food that was to nourish it*
*was ever prepared by you to satisfy all our desires.*
*As our strength increased, our tasks were ready for us.*

# Haunted by Strange Shadows
## Acts 17:22-27

*So that they might seek God,*
*if perhaps they might feel after him and find him,*
*though he is not far from every one of us.*
(verse 27, Montgomery)

The mere fact that all over the world
  human beings have had a religion of some kind,
    that they have groped through the darkness for a God
      whom they felt to be near,
  is a serious and pathetic fact.
It is as if the race had nearly lost one of its senses
    or else not yet fully acquired it,
  and was haunted by strange shadows,
    calling and beckoning with chills of terror
      or thrills of blessedness,
    telling of a marvelous world lying close to us,
      and yet almost out of reach.

*O God, from afar comes your mysterious call to the ear of our spirit.*
*Amid the din of the market, amid the shout of our companions,*
*or in the silence of our chamber*
*we hear it and we know that you are near*
*and that we are face to face with our real destiny.*

# An Aid to Revelation

## John 5:36-40

*You are searching the scriptures*
*because you suppose that in them you have eternal life.*
(verse 39, Montgomery)

In the Bible we have the record of the revelations of God to holy ones;
    their visions of the character of God;
    their inspired interpretations of history;
    and their outlooks into God's purposes for the future.
But it must not be forgotten that the Bible
    is only in a secondary sense "revelation,"
    it is the result of revelation
    and in turn an aid to revelation,
but revelation in the closest sense of the word is always
    an act of the living God,
    a personal contact between God's spirit and the human spirit,
whereby the latter is quickened and enlightened.

*O God, we thank you for the beauty and attractiveness of wisdom,*
*for truly it is more precious than silver*
*and more satisfying than any outward possessions.*
*We thank you that you have made us to taste its sweetness*
*and have put into our souls a hunger for knowledge*
*that can never again be quenched.*

# All the Universe a Revelation of God
## Psalm 19:1-6

*The heavens are telling the glory of God,*
*and the firmament proclaims his handiwork.*

There is a large sense in which all the universe
  is a revelation of God.
The starry heavens tell of his infinitude;
the cataracts are his voices;
the sunbeams his messengers of love;
the immutable laws of nature
  are solemn preachers of his justice;
and even the eggshell thrown from the robin's nest
  testifies to his wisdom.
Since the creation of the world, as Paul says,
  the invisible character of God,
    God's everlasting power and godhead,
  has been discerned through God's visible works.
The rain that has moistened the fields,
  the food that has filled our hearts with gladness,
    have been witnesses to God.

*O Lord, you are infinite in power and majesty.*
*We look up at the starry heavens and our imagination grows dizzy*
*as we try to think of the vast reaches of space.*
*Yet you who makes the heavens your habitation*
*are ready to dwell in the contrite human heart.*
*We are the real home that you desire.*

# Learn to Know God
## Colossians 1:15-20

*He is the likeness of the unseen God.*
(verse 15, Goodspeed)

To us who regard Jesus as the unique revelation of God,
    the unfolding of the divine life under human forms,
  he is the ultimate standard of moral and spiritual life,
  the perfect expression of the will of God for humanity,
  the categorical imperative with a human heart.
Christ excels the former revelations
    because he imposes no outward law…
  There is no legalism in him.
  He writes his law on our hearts.
When we have come to know Christ
  the law is…an impulse within,
    which lifts us and in which we glory…
No one need say to another:
  "Sit thou down here and I will teach thee to know God."
Now we take our brother and sister by the hand
  and bring them to meet Jesus,
  and there they learn to know God
  by the secret intuitions of love
  and the molding touches of fellowship.

*O Lord, we beseech you to save us*
*from the narrowness of pride and self-satisfied isolation*
*by which we bar you out*
*and make ourselves our spiritual universe.*

# True Christianity

## John 20:24-28

*We have seen the Master!*
*(verse 25, Goodspeed)*

True Christianity puts one face to face with Christ
   and bids that person see what she or he can find there.
And if they do not fall down at once and hail him with Thomas:
     "My Lord and my God," (John 20:28),
   but simply tell of a man surpassing strong and tender,
   we bid them keep on looking.
And slowly the blurring mist of worldliness
   will drop from their eyes,
   and their soul will become capable of measuring
   the stature of Jesus among mortals,
and it may be that they will echo the experience of a great disciple:
   "The Word became flesh and dwelt among us;
   and we gazed upon his glory,
   and found it to be a glory as of the only begotten from the Father,
   full of grace and truth."

*O Jesus, help us to dare the assertion*
*that we too are children of God,*
*offspring of the Eternal, spirit of God's Spirit.*

# The Writings of John
## John 20:30-31

*These have been written that you may believe that Jesus is the Christ*
*and have life in his name.*
(verse 31, Montgomery)

There is something in the writings of John,
    —their style, their thought, the spirit that pervades them—
  which distinguishes them from the other writers of the New Testament.
John sees truth and expresses it in a way peculiar to himself.
    The events that occur in time seem to have no interest for him,
    save as they are the manifestations of timeless principles.
It is these eternal principles that he lays bare;
    them he traces up and down and through
        the whole length and breadth of the spiritual universe.
As Newton formulated a simple law,
        the application of which explains both
        why the constellations keep on in their courses
        and why the feather floats in the air,
  so John states and re-states a few great and all-pervading laws
      of the moral and religious world.
His theme is the antagonism of truth and lie,
      the conflict of light and darkness,
      the struggle of life and death,
  and these words,
        the symbols of his great ideas,
      meet us everywhere on these pages,
staggering along under the burden of thought
      that he has loaded upon them.

*Give us, we pray, the heart of a little child,*
*simple, trustful, cheerful, loving,*
*that thus we may be put in the way of receiving*
*that higher wisdom which is revealed*
*only to the childlike and hidden from the wise.*

# The Eternal Life
## John 17:3

*Eternal life means knowing you as the only true God,*
*And knowing Jesus your messenger as Christ.*
(Goodspeed)

One of John's constantly recurring expressions is "the eternal life."
In the other writers of the New Testament
   this expression refers, almost without exception,
     to the life after death.
In John, on the contrary,
   the passages are rare in which it has a distinct reference
     to the future life.
With John it is the life lived *now*
   by all those who have believed
     and have thereby passed from death into life.
When John calls this life "the eternal life,"
   he describes not so much its duration as its character;
   it is a life not of this world,
a spiritual, a divine life,
   and by virtue of that character
     it is also an endless life,
for no death of the flesh can kill the spirit.
*"And this is eternal life"*

*We praise you that you have sustained and built up our spiritual life.*
*You have not suffered us to come into temptations*
*that would have overpowered us,*
*and to slip away down the icy chasms*
*of doubt and despair.*

# Eternal Life Is New Life
## John 12:25, 44-46

*Those who love their life lose it;*
*and those who regard not their life in this world*
*shall keep it for eternal life.*
(verse 25, Montgomery)

"The eternal life" is
  a new life,
    in which the believer lives
    and which lives in the believer;
  a life nourished by new and spiritual powers;
  a life even now in communication with the life beyond,
    governed by its laws and run in its molds.
What Peter calls
  "being begotten again unto a living hope";
what James designates as
  "receiving with weakness the implanted word";
what Paul characterizes as
  being justified and created anew,
  all that is expressed by John in the words:
    "the eternal life."

*O God, make us fit to house the Lord of Glory.*
*May Christ be no homeless wanderer,*
*so far as we are concerned,*
*but may he find in us a resting place and temple.*

# Knowledge and the Eternal Life
## 1 John 2:3-6

*This is how we may know that we have come to know Jesus Christ,*
*by always keeping his commandments.*
(verse 3, Montgomery)

What satisfaction is it to God,
   when a person proves that there is a God
   and then lives as if there is none?
It is the heart that God looks to;
   it is the Christlike life that God wants.
Any knowledge that does not operate
   to make the heart purer and better
   is not the knowledge that belongs to the eternal life....
Obedience to God is the test of the true knowledge of God.
   Again: "Those that love not, know not God, for God is love."
Here a heart that is full of love
   is the test of the true knowledge of God.
A knowledge that is not wedded to love and prolific in action
   is not the knowledge that belongs
      to the eternal life.

*We bless you above all things for the light*
*that has come into our life through Jesus Christ;*
*not in fitful vision, not in passing splendor like the flash of lightning,*
*but in the steady shining of the sun of righteousness,*
*in the white light of a life that was filled with God.*

# Knowledge that Dominates Affections and Will
## 1 John 5:13-20

*We know that the Son of God is come, and has granted us an understanding,*
*so that we may come to him who is true.*
(verse 20, Montgomery)

Every shred of knowledge in our possession
   must become operative in our life,
      else it profits us nothing.
It must be changed from the inorganic to the organic;
   it must be assimilated into our spiritual organism
      and not till then
      does it become part of that knowledge
      which is the eternal life in us....
This knowledge which is life eternal
   must be a knowledge that is not dependent
      on natural brightness
      or acquired training of the reasoning faculties;
   and it must be a knowledge that is in immediate connection
      with our affections and will
         and dominates them.

*O Jesus, may we never mistake*
*the bitterness of our own passion for the zeal of God.*
*Grant us your gentle spirit and unite it*
*with your spirit of courage and devotion to your Father's will.*

# Turning Knowledge to Conviction
## 3 John 2-4

*I have no greater joy than this, to hear that my children
are passing their lives in the truth.*
(verse 4, Montgomery)

The mere external knowledge of any truth in you
   will turn to conviction in you
     as you bring that truth into your life
     and cry to God for help in doing so.
Cease to live up to a conviction
   and to pray over it,
   and your conviction will fade into mere knowledge.
The knowledge of which we speak, then,
   is not a single mental act,
     it is rather a constant activity,
        and not of the intellect only,
        but of one's whole soul....
Every exercise of this knowledge,
   every renewed contemplation of divine truth
     and obedience to it
   nourishes and intensifies the divine life in us.

*If there is any sin unsurrendered,
help us to thrust it out
to wither in the light of your presence.*

# The Measure of the Eternal Life in Us
## John 14:18-21

*Because I shall live on, and you will live on too.*
(verse 19, Goodspeed)

It would be of small importance to us
   actually to conceive of God as being everywhere,
      even if it were possible to us.
It is of the very greatest importance for our spiritual life
   that we have a profound sense
   of God's presence with us at all times,
      knowing that God's eye is ever fixed upon us,
      knowing that God hears at this moment
         every word that is spoken
         and every quickening heartbeat that answers to it;
      knowing too that if we should go to dwell
         on the other side of the earth,
         God's hand shall still lead us
         and God's right hand hold us.
To believe God just in his judgments and not arbitrary,
   to trust God as compassionate and not merciless,
   to love God as one who loves us
      and is not a heartless and passionless force,
   that does concern us,
      and the measure of our living conviction on that
         is also the measure of the eternal life in us.

*You have poured out the spirit of adoption into our hearts*
*that yearns to you in love and calls you Father.*
*Now we obey you not from fear but from love.*

# We Small Creatures Know God?
## John 1:16-18

*No one has ever seen God.*
(verse 18, Goodspeed)

Friends, I do believe that Christ meant what he said,
  when he told us that no one had seen God at any time
    except the Son.
We persist in believing the contrary.
We toss about the words "infinite," "eternal,"
  "omniscient," "omnipresent,"
    —as if we knew what they mean!
We pile them up as children do their toy blocks,
  and then step aside to admire
    the God that we have constructed.
We—small creatures on a tiny star!—know God?
We, who measure time by a succession of seconds,
  know the One to whom a single day is as a thousand years
    and a thousand years brief as a day?
Go, lay your hand on the earth and say,
  "O earth, I hold thee! I weigh thee in my hand and know thee!"
  and you will give others an image of someone who says, "I know God."
We cannot know God as God is…

*O Jesus, Son of God,*
*lift us to like faith with you in the Father*
*who has counted the hairs on our head*
*and holds us dear.*

# The Only God Whom We Can Know
## John 1:16-18

*It is the divine Only Son, who leans upon the Father's breast,*
*that has made God known.*
(verse 18, Goodspeed)

We cannot know God as God is
  and God knows that we cannot.
When God revealed himself in Christ,
    God revealed himself in the one way
      in which we can know God.
The Word became flesh and dwelt among us.
The only God whom we can know is a human God,
   with a heart that answers to our heart,
   who loves as we love,
   who is angry as we are angry,
   who sorrows with our griefs
     and rejoices with our joys.
Take away from our God the human heart,
  and God becomes cold, distant,
    and without power over our hearts....
If we would know God,
  we must see God revealed in the flesh.

*O God, you have made our lives so rich in the highest things.*
*You have given us yourself, the greatest wealth of all,*
*and Jesus Christ, our Savior and Lord,*
*who has transformed our life and will yet glorify it.*

# Knowing Christ Is Knowing God
## John 14:8-10

*Whoever has seen me has seen the Father.*
(verse 9, Montgomery)

We cannot know God as God is;
   but if we know Christ, we know the Father;
   we know the Father in the measure in which we know Christ.
If we gaze upon Christ,
   we shall behold his glory and feel that it is the glory
     as of the only begotten from the Father, full of grace and truth.
In him burns the divine light;
   the screen of flesh tempers it to our weak eyes.
The eye that turns not away from it
   but delights in its radiance
will grow stronger to endure it;
   and as it grows stronger, the light will grow brighter.
If we are willing to follow him, we shall never walk in darkness;
   the hour will never come
when we will outstrip our torchbearer,
when we will say to Christ,
   "You have no more to give me; I need you no longer."
Christ will still be before us,
   still revealing to us
     whatever God we are capable of receiving.

*Almighty God, our heavenly Father,*
*in knowledge of whom stands our eternal life,*
*whose service is perfect freedom,*
*grant that through your blessed Son we may know you as are you are*
*and learn to serve you wisely in our generation.*

# Eternal Life Pouring into Our Hearts
## John 7:37-38

*...rivers of living water...*
(verse 38, Montgomery)

If we learn to know Christ,
   not his words alone
      which are but a partial expression of him,
   but him,
   the man Jesus Christ;
if our practice presses close at the heels of our knowledge,
   and we thus know him as only like knows like,
then we shall find the very life eternal
   pouring into our hearts,
      as the sea at high tide
         pushes up into every cove and inlet.

*O God, you are light and in you is no darkness.*
*Your life is the light of all people.*
*You enfold us all in your brightness,*
*and if our souls are dark*
*it is because we have kept you out.*

# This Is Indeed the Life Eternal
## John 21:12-18

*Do you love me? Do you love me? Am I really dear to you?*
(Montgomery)

O the riches of a life with Christ,
a life in which the human Savior
   is ever present,
   comforting, admonishing, helping;
a life that glows with love for him;
a life in which all thoughts turn to him
   as the atoms in the iron turn to the magnet;
a life that is like a well
   filled to the brim with pure water,
     and overflows constantly
     with spontaneous acts of charity and helpfulness.
Those that live such a life know God;
   they know God through Jesus Christ;
   and the life that they live is the eternal life.
The knowledge will nourish the life,
   and the life being strengthened will make us ready for greater knowledge.
They grow together;
   every day it will be truer than it ever was before,
that this is indeed the life eternal
   to know the only true God, and him who has been sent, Jesus Christ.

*May your light burn so brightly in us*
*that the tongues of fire can leap from us to others.*

# Learn from Madam Guyon
## Ephesians 1:3-5

*...who has blessed us in every spiritual blessing
in the heavenly realms in Christ.*
(verse 3, Montgomery)

...a woman whose genius compels our admiration,
   whose sad history obtains our compassion,
     and whose fervid piety may persuade us to imitation.
We speak of Madame Guyon.
Her life was a remarkable one.
She lived in France, the land of wit and superficiality,
   and her life was hid with Christ in God....
She was passionately revered by some
   and as passionately reviled by many.
Her body languished for years in the dungeons of the Bastille
   while her soul was in the presence of God....
She was simultaneously revered as a saint,
   and persecuted as a heretic....
At last, cleared of all personal charges,
   she was permitted to live quietly among those who loved her,
   and to await in a peaceful old age
     the last command of the One whom she had delighted to obey.

*We bless you for our own fathers and mothers in the faith,
for the godly pastors who awakened our souls,
for the aged servants of Jesus who gave us their smile and benediction.
O Master, give us grace to follow in their train.*

This and the next eight reflections are from Walter Rauschenbusch's unpublished manuscript, "Madame Guyon." Jeanne Guyon (1648–1717) was a French Christian mystic. Rauschenbusch's handwritten notes at the end of the manuscript indicate: "Written for the class in homiletics (Dr. T. H. Patterson) as a study of a devotional writer in the Middle or Senior year, 1884-6. 1894 I recast the beginning and end for the New York Ministers Conference.... Read to senior class, 1906."

# Embrace the Good Thing Despite the Excesses
## Ephesians 3:14-19

*...from whom every family in heaven or on earth takes its name.*
(verse 14, Goodspeed)

It would be easy to point out the dangerous consequences
  that might flow
    from the dangerous teaching of Madam Guyon....
But it is not fair to charge a system with all the evil
  that might follow from it
    if it were pressed to its extreme consequences
      without the ballast of common sense
        and the restraining influence of society and custom
        and the protecting hand of God.
Why, even Calvinism might possibly lead to unsaintly consequences.
It is true that Madam Guyon teaches a loss of personality
  and an absorption into God which makes us pause....
But the harmful excess of a good thing
  ought not to make us reject the good thing itself.

*We thank you for the churches that nurtured us*
*and offered us the fellowship of godly men and women;*
*for the pastors who inspired and comforted us;*
*for the friends who shared with us their own yearnings and so led us on;*
*for the books that were the fruit of holy lives and a Christ-like will;*
*for every passing message that came hot to our hearts*
*because your Spirit sent it.*

# Restless Souls
## Ephesians 3:14-19

*…your inmost being…*
(verse 6, Montgomery)

The souls of mortals are ever restless;
they are restless because
   they have not yet returned to God,
     their origin.
They are like the water that rises in mist from the ocean;
though it falls as rain high on the mountains,
   straightway it starts for its home,
     the sea,
        by brooklet and creek and river.
And as among the streams
   there are some that flow along quietly,
     others that run swiftly,
       and still others that rush down headlong,
         so it is with the souls of mortals.

*Teach us the blessed art of rest in God.*
*Increase our longings for your presence,*
*so that we may have times*
*when we faint with desire for the courts of God,*
*and that like the swallow*
*we may find our nesting-place where you are near.*

# Heartbeats

## Ephesians 3:14-19

*...praying that Christ make his home in your hearts through your faith...*
(verse 17, Montgomery)

If we lift up our hearts,
   let us keep our feet on the ground.
If we lose our souls in rapture,
   let us not lose from our actions
     the plain moralities of life.
Let us not be among those
   who use high words about the union with Christ,
     but whose life drops with unkind judgments,
     whose eyes flash jealousy,
     and whose walk is in places
       where none could follow save with tears and shame.
Let us learn from the life of Madam Guyon
   that it is possible for our hearts to beat in time
     with the great heart of God,
and for our wills to will in harmony with God's will
   to a degree of which we have but little conception.

*Your will is the only pathway to enduring joy;*
*help us to choose your will.*
*Teach us to be humble in heart,*
*but to ask at the hand of the king*
*some splendid quest that will take all our powers.*

# Seek, Yield, Keep Open, Press Onward

## Ephesians 3:14-19

*…deeply rooted and firmly grounded in love.*
(verse 17, Montgomery)

We can learn from Madam Guyon
   not to rest content with the gifts,
     but to seek the Giver;
to yield our will in order that we
   may know and do God's will;
to keep our minds open to the light divine
   and our souls plastic to the touch of God;
to be content with no reflected radiance
   but to press onward unceasingly
     to the presence of the One
        who is ever unseen
     and yet ever present.

*Your will has become our will,*
*and our duty has become our joy.*
*The strange constraining power of your life in us*
*sustains our faltering will.*

# Eternal Tendencies in the Human Soul
## Ephesians 3:14-19

*…comprehend with all the saints…*
(verse 18, Montgomery)

There is a marvelous diversity in the forms of religious life,
   and a marvelous stability and uniformity in the life itself.
The mountains of New England are not honeycombed
   with cavernous dwellings that echo
      to the falling of the scourge and the groans of the ascetic,
   as was Mount Sinai, twelve centuries ago.
The beatific visions that darkened with their ineffable brightness
   the convent cell of the mystic,
      no longer visit our studies.
And yet, in spite of the apparent dissimilarity,
      it would not be difficult to find in the religious life of today
   types quite analogous to those which gaze at us
   with so weird a look from the pages of religious history.
They were manifestations of eternal tendencies in the human soul.

*O God, there is none so far away from you*
*but that some of your sweet light*
*enters into that soul*
*and bears testimony to itself and to you.*

# Not All of Christianity

## Ephesians 3:14-19

*...comprehend what is "the breadth," "the length," "the depth," and "the height"...*
(verse 18, Montgomery)

A redemption for us is not all of Christianity;
a decree of justification that forgiveness
   is passed on our behalf is not all;
a revelation historically given
   and deposited in a book is not all;
participation in the life and worship of the Church
   is not the greatest possible nearness to God.
It is possible to deal with God himself;
to speak to God and to listen to God;
to receive rays of light that are broken by no human prism
   but that come directly from the throne of glory;
it is possible to have leadings in our life
   that are not the utterances of common sense
     nor the advice of human friends,
but the impulses of the great unseen hand of our Father.

*O God, give us courage to press on*
*and follow the truth as you show it,*
*even if loving voices warn us back.*
*Only, Lord, suffer us not to go astray permanently*
*by mistaking the fleeting whispers of our own passions*
*for the eternal word of God,*
*or by following wandering lights that lead to destruction.*

# It Is Possible

## Ephesians 3:14-19

*...understanding Christ's love, so far beyond our understanding...*
(verse 19, Goodspeed)

Such is the inner life with God
  which Madam Guyon would have us lead.
And would we not fain believe that it is possible?
The traveler in the heat and dust of the plain
  looks up longingly to the white stillness of the Alpine peak,
    clad eternally with virgin snow
      bathed in the purest air,
      and holding conversation with the stars.
That is a truth in mysticism.
Paul's Christianity was not obedience to a book outside him,
  but obedience to a Spirit within him.
He was sensible of the merging
  of the Paul-life and the Christ-life,
    so that he lived no longer,
      but Christ lived in him.
John believed that we have the Son of God
  and having him we have his life within us,
    and also an anointing so that we know all things.

*O Master, our own work seems puny and selfish compared with Paul's.*
*But Paul's God is our God, and Paul's Master is our Master,*
*and as you were able to do great things through him*
*because your life filled him wholly,*
*so you will yet do great things through us,*
*though we are but bruised reeds in our own sight.*

# There Are Still Ardent Hearts
## Ephesians 3:14-19

*...so that you may be filled with the very fullness of God.*
(verse 19, Goodspeed)

Mysticism has not died out among us,
   nor can it die.
There are still ardent hearts,
   impatient of the slow, toiling ascent
     of a faithful, humble Christian life;
hearts that long for some mighty sanctifying power
   to carry them, as with the sweep of an eagle's pinions,
     out of the depressed,
       up-and-down experience
         of the average Christian
     into the clear air of a higher life with God.
There are still some who would fain
   draw aside the veil of the finite
     and attempt to behold the Infinite One face to face.

*O God, you have been*
*at our right hand and our left,*
*before us and behind us,*
*above us and below us,*
*about us and within us,*
*and every fiber of our mystic nature*
*has been aquiver with God.*

# A Power Direct from the Unseen World
## Romans 8:26-27

*The Spirit takes hold of us in our weakness.*
(verse 26, Montgomery)

In aftertimes Christianity came to mean largely
  creeds, rituals, rules, holy buildings and priests—
    a sort of religion at second hand
      with a reflected light and warmth.
But in the first generation it came over people
  as a power direct from the unseen world;
  as a new and sweet vitality
    that melted their hearts with a glow of divine love
    and overwhelmed the baser passions of the past;
  as a revelation and vision…,
    creating an insight and foresight…,
    inspiring prayers and longings
      so intense and lofty
  they seemed to hear God's own spirit
  groaning in travail within their breasts.

*O God, may we be so wholly consecrated to you,*
*and so purely enlightened by you,*
*that you can safely entrust the greater powers of your Spirit to us,*
*lest we misuse your Spirit*
*to smite in our anger*
*or to adorn ourselves in our vainglory.*

# A Cry of Need
## Psalm 130 and Matthew 6:5-8

*Out of the depths I cry to you, O Lord!*
*Lord, hear my voice!* (Ps 130:1-2)

Heart religion is always a cry of need.
People pray because of a burden in their life;
   sickness threatens them;
   a child is in danger;
   some morbid passion has gained footing
      in their mind or body and can not be shaken off;
   some evil has been done which cannot be undone.
The need is beyond their own strength.
So they cry to a higher Power
   to help,
   to forgive,
   to cleanse,
   to save.
I believe in the victorious power of the spiritual life.
Faith can overcome the world
   and glory even in tribulation.
I have seen holy lives unfolding
   in the most depressing surrounding,
      like Edelweiss at the edge of a glacier.

*O God, bless the sick and those whose strength is spent and weary.*
*Bless the lonely who have lost some dear heart*
   *for which they long in vain,*
   *and those other lonely ones*
*whose life has never been made rich by love.*

# The Profoundest Classification of People
## Luke 18:9-14

*Two men were going up to the Temple to pray;*
*the one a Pharisee, the other a tax-gatherer.*
(verse 10, Montgomery)

People can be classified in many ways.
You can classify them as rich and poor,
   as strong and weak,
   as capable and stupid,
   as moral and immoral.
But perhaps one of the profoundest classifications
   would be the division between
     those who truly pray and those who do not.
There is a great difference between them,
   both for their personal happiness
     and for their influence and power in life.

*Our Father, grant us faith in prayer.*
*There are times when our faith droops.*
*When the universe and the stars come over us,*
*and all things seem to come by nature,*
*it is hard for us to believe that the God*
*whose power upholds the constellations*
*can care for the cry of puny mortals such as we.*

# A Strange Sweetness
## Mark 6:45-52

*After he had taken leave of them,*
*he went away into the mountain to pray.*
(verse 46, Montgomery)

There is a strange sweetness in real prayer,
   when you are conscious of touching God.
There are many joys in life:
      the relish of youth and health,
      the joy of learning,
      the thrill of love;
   but is any of them quite like the joy of prayer?
Any one who has ever experienced it,
   will always be haunted by homesickness for it.
It surpasses other pleasures, not only in degree, but in kind.
It does not pall.
It does not lash us on with the desire for some satisfaction
   which seems always just ahead
   and yet always eludes us.
It is inexpressibly satisfying while it lasts;
   every renewal of it is good;
   there is always more ahead,
   and yet we are strangely content with what we have.
It combines desire and satisfaction, progress and rest.

*O God, you have blessed us a thousand times beyond our deserts.*
*Often we have forgotten you;*
*sometimes we have directly disobeyed you*
*and denied you in our life.*
*But you have ever been*
*faithful, patient, and full of glorious lovingkindness.*

# The Ifs of Prayer

## Luke 11:1-4

*Master, teach us to pray.*
(verse 1, Goodspeed)

If the effect of our prayers
   goes beyond our own personality;
if there is a center of the spiritual universe
   in whom our spirits join and have their being;
and if the mysterious call of our souls
   somehow reaches and moves God,
     so that our language comes back from God
       in a wave of divine assent
       which assures their ultimate fulfillment—
then it may mean more than any one knows
   to set Christendom praying on our social problems.

*We need you, O great enlarger of our souls,*
*and we would through the portals of our spirit open to you.*
*We would make wide and high the gates*
*that the King of Glory may enter in.*

# A Breathing Space
## Luke 19:41-44

*When Jesus came into view of the city, as he approached it,*
*he broke into loud weeping.*
(verse 41, Montgomery)

When we are
in the presence of God,
   the best that is in us
   has a breathing space.
Then, if ever, we feel
    the vanity
    and shamefulness
   of much that society calls
   proper and necessary.
If we had more prayer in common
    on the sins of modern society,
   there would be more social repentance
   and less angry resistance
    to the demands of justice and mercy.

*O God, we pray you make our lives rich*
*in all the graces of a holy life.*
*May we abound in love and gentleness,*
*in helpfulness and hospitality,*
*in purity and truthfulness.*
*May there be no uncleanness in our act,*
*nor in our conversation,*
*nor in our secret thoughts and imaginations.*

# Prayer and Morality
## Matthew 5:43-48

*Love your enemies, and pray for your persecutors.*
(verse 44, Goodspeed)

Prayer transforms mere information
  into will and conviction,
    and deepens the sense of duty.
Prayer is the most distinctively religious act.
Morality is the outcome of religion;
  it is the test of religion; but it is not religion itself.
A person may be just and loving,
  but if that person does not pray,
  she or he lacks something in the sight of God
  and lacks something in the depth of one's own consciousness
    that would give
      a stronger sweep to one's soul,
      a rare fragrance to one's love,
      a braver poise to one's walk.

*O bow our stubborn and unwilling hearts*
*that we may give up to you our dearest sins*
*and grant your Spirit a free and complete work within us,*
*to search us and prove us and cleanse us and make us holy.*

# Emotionless Spirituality Is Valueless
## Psalm 103:1-5

*Bless the Lord, O my soul,*
*and all that is within me,*
*bless his holy name.*
(verse 1)

A religion without emotion
  is valueless.
Preaching without emotion
  has no saving power.
Being saved without emotion
  is unthinkable.
If I had to choose between intellect and emotion
  in religious work,
I would rather have genuine emotion
  with little intellect
  than the reverse.
In mathematics or the natural science
I might prefer the person with cold, clear
  and unbiased intellect,
but in Christian life and Christian work,
I would rather have genuine emotion
  with little intellect
than great intellect
  with little emotion.

*O Lord, may we feel deeply our dependence on you*
*and ever walk humbly in your sight.*

# Talk Out as You Feel
## Mark 3:1-6

*...looking around upon them with anger,*
*and deeply grieved by the hardness of their hearts.*
(verse 5, Montgomery)

Emotion is good only when it is spontaneous,
  only when it rises naturally in the soul.
So I should say:
  Never strive after emotion when you do not feel it;
but, on the other hand,
  never restrain emotion if you do feel it.
Be genuine. Talk out as you feel.
And keep clear of any environment
  which would check a good and genuine emotion.
If anybody tried to put me in one of those old barrel pulpits
  and swaddle me in a gown
  in which I could not move my arms freely,
    I should certainly tear something.
I want to have a chance to express all genuine emotion
  which the Lord awakens in me.

*O God, we thank you for the strength we draw*
*from the backward look and the thought of bygone years.*
*We bless you for the deep sense of your presence*
*that comes over us as we contemplate the course of our lives.*
*For you have been with us from the beginning.*

# Re-establishing the Teachings of Jesus
## Colossians 3:12-17

*Let the message of Christ have life in your hearts in all its wealth of wisdom.*
*(verse 16, Goodspeed)*

When I was a young man of twenty,
   the thought began to hold mastery over my mind
      that I must live over again the life of Jesus,
         and if necessary die over again his death in some way.
I have not lived up to that,
   but that purpose gave my life its fundamental direction.
When I began to have some insight into the social questions,
   and to realize how deeply the teachings of Jesus differed
      from the teachings ordinarily accepted in the Church,
I dedicated myself to the task of re-establishing
   the teachings of Jesus Christ
      in the common thought of the Church,
   and of establishing his precepts
      as the common principles of the social world.
Whatever good there has been in my life has been on these lines.

*Help us, O God, to follow in the footsteps of the Master*
*and to prepare for our service*
*by taking upon us the utter yoke of obedience.*

# The Final Word for Christian Minds
## Luke 6:46-49

*Why are you calling me, Lord, Lord, and not doing what I tell you?*
(verse 46, Montgomery)

Jesus, to me, has the final word for Christian minds.
Others may look at him, as they like,
   but to us who have taken the vow of discipleship,
     he is the Master and the Lord.
In the early Church,
   Christ was given a unique position of authority.
He was the Master,
   and none of the disciples would have dared
     to rank their own words with the words of Jesus.
In later times the doctrine of inspiration
   neutralized his peculiar position
     and ranked the others on the same level of inspired infallibility.
I believe we ought to go back to the apostolic practice
   and rank Jesus above all others.

*Grant us the grace of a quiet and humble mind*
*and help us to learn of Jesus*
*to be meek and lowly of heart,*
*that we may find rest for our souls.*

# The Rarest Secret of All
## John 10:7-10

*I have come to let them have life, and to let them have it in abundance.*
(verse 10, Goodspeed)

Jesus had learned the greatest and deepest and rarest secret of all—
   how to live a religious life....
Beyond the question of economic distribution
     lies that question of moral relations;
   and beyond the moral relations to others
     lies the question of the religious communion
     with that spiritual reality in which
     we live and move and have our deepest being—
     with God, the Father of our spirits.
Jesus had realized the life of God in the human soul
   and the life of humans in the love of God.
That was the real secret of his life,
   the well-spring of his purity,
     his compassion,
     his unwearied courage,
     his unquenchable idealism:
        he knew the Father.

*O God, we have felt that attractiveness*
*of the light, the love, the tenderness, the compassion of Jesus,*
*and we care not to go elsewhere,*
*for we have believed that he is*
*your Christ and the Son of God.*
*And we who receive him are becoming*
*children of God through him.*

# Sharing the Secret
## John 15:1-17

*I have made known to you everything that I have learned from my Father.*
(verse 15, Goodspeed)

If Jesus had that greatest of all possessions,
    the key to the secret of life,
  it was his highest social duty to share it
  and help others to gain what he had.
He had to teach others to live
    as children in the presence of the Father,
    and no longer as slaves cringing before a despot.
He had to show them that the ordinary life
    of selfishness and hate
    and anxiety and chafing ambition and covetousness
  is no life at all and that they must enter into a new world
    of love and solidarity and inward contentment.
There was no service that he could render
  which would equal that.
All other help lay in concentric circles
  about that redemption of the spirit
  and flowed out from it.

*O God, we beseech you to save us*
*from the distractions and sorrows of vanity*
*and inordinate ambition.*

# The Deceitfulness of Riches
## Matthew 13:22

*...but the anxieties of the age and the deceitfulness of riches choke the word, and it becomes unfruitful.*
(Montgomery)

Like the greatest spiritual teachers,
   Jesus realized a profound danger to the better self
      in the pursuit of wealth.
Whoever will watch the development of a soul
   that has bent its energies to the task of becoming rich,
      can see how perilous the process is
   to the finer sense of justice,
   to the instinct of mercy and kindness and equality,
   and to the singleness of devotion to higher ends;
   in short, to all the higher humanity in us.
It is a simple fact: "Ye cannot serve God and mammon;"
   each requires the best of a person.
"The cares of this life and the deceitfulness of riches"—
     note that quality of deceitfulness—
   will choke the good seed like rank weeds
     which appropriate soil and sunshine for their own growth....
Wealth is apt to grow stronger than the person who owns it.
It owns the person
   and that person loses one's moral and spiritual freedom....
And the worst of it is that the person does not know it.

*O God, save us and our service*
*from self-seeking and the love of money.*
*Grant us day by day our daily bread*
*for ourselves and for those dependent on us,*
*and make us content.*

# Those Jesus Ridiculed

## Matthew 23:23-28

*Woe unto you Scribes and Pharisees, hypocrites!*
*(verses 23, 25, 27, Montgomery)*

Jesus ridiculed the models of piety
   who were so punctilious about ritual observances
   and so indifferent to wrong moral relations.
They faithfully gave a tithe of everything to religion,
   down to the mint, anise, and cummin in their garden bed,
   but such little things as justice and mercy and good faith,
     the qualities on which human society rests
     and which constitute the real burden of the Law,
   they quite overlooked.
When Jesus saw a Pharisee straining the milk
   lest haply he should swallow a drowned gnat
   and so transgress the Law in eating a strangled beast,
   he saw there a type of what these religious men
     were doing all the time:
     straining out gnats and swallowing camels.
They wiped the outside of the platter,
   but within it was "filled with extortion and excess";
     their food was acquired by injustice and consumed in luxury.
They even nullified the fundamental obligation
   of the child to the parent by teaching
     that if a person gave money to the temple,
     and thus supported the ritual worship of God,
   that person was free from the duty of supporting the parents.
Thus religion had become a parasite in the body of morality
   and was draining it instead of feeding it.

*Our Father, accept the humble acknowledgement of our sins.*
*We have nothing to be proud of.*
*What have we that you have not first given to us?*
*Even our righteousnesses are spotted and stained*
*with our selfishness and vainglory.*
*All our confidence is in you alone.*

# The Reign of Hate
## 1 Corinthians 13:4-8

*Love bears no malice, never rejoices over wrong-doing,*
*but rejoices when the truth rejoices.*
(verses 5-6, Montgomery)

The reign of hate concerns Christianity
   more than anything else about the war.
Christianity is based on love as the supreme law.
As long as we love,
   we are on the way of salvation and will come right.
As long as we hate,
   we are on the way of damnation, and all will go wrong.
What are the functions of Christianity in a world
     drugged and crazy with hate? ...
Naturally the hate of one nation for another
   is different than the hate of one individual for another,
     more deadly but less personal.
In his characterization of love, Paul says, "Love thinks no evil."
   It takes the best view possible;
   it watches against misunderstandings
   and is critical when any evil is spoken
     against the person loved.
Hate, on the other hand, is eager to believe the worst
    and reluctant to believe anything good.
  You can't convince it that the hated person has any virtues.
Hate breeds lies. It runs to slander as a duck takes to the water.

*Save us from blighting the fresh flower of any heart*
*by the flare of sudden anger or secret hate.*
*May we not bruise the rightful self-respect of any*
*by contempt or malice.*

# What Hate Really Is
## Ephesians 4:25–5:1

*Banish from among you all bitterness and passion and clamor and slander,*
*as well as malice.*
(verse 31, Montgomery)

Hate takes different forms when it looks up
    and when it looks down.
  Toward the strong it takes the form of resentment,
    readiness to surmise an insult,
      refusal to be put upon.
  Toward the weak hate takes the form of contempt....
Hate rejoices in the injury of the other.
Bad tidings for the other are good tidings.
Judged by that, is there any hate in the world today?
I think these are some of the chief symptoms of hate:
    willingness to think evil and to lie;
    fear;
    resentment;
    contempt;
    satisfaction in the injury of another.
If I meet this state of mind
  I should certainly not say
  that such a person
  was in a state of Christian love and peace.

*We pray you to break the oppression of fear*
*that has cowed even the good and the brave in our cities.*

# The Real Thing
## Proverbs 4:18-23

*The path of the righteous is like the light of dawn,*
*which shines brighter and brighter until full day.*
(verse 18)

To exploit no one and to love every one,
to be at peace with your brother and sister
   and with yourself and with your God,
to sing with joy at sight of a sunset
   or an autumn creeper or a happy child,
to prize truth and knowledge,
to turn effortless from thought to adoration,
and to enjoy prayer as the highest exercise of life
—this is the real thing;
   the rest is scaffolding.

*Our Father, day by day*
*we gather for our sacrifice of adoration.*
*We sing your praises.*
*We speak to you in prayer.*
*We beseech you that our service*
*may not be with vain repetitions,*
*meaningless to you and useless to ourselves.*
*May the sound of our prayers*
*not beat against these walls,*
*but may the still small voice of the soul's desire*
*reach you and call you.*

# Keep Moving Forward
## Proverbs 4:24-27

*Keep straight the path of your feet, and all your ways will be sure.*
(verse 26)

We are all moving in a different spiritual world,
  and in a different moral atmosphere than ten years ago.
If that is not true of any individuals,
  may God have mercy on them,
    for they are missing their chance at salvation.
The life of religion is always in its forward movements,
  as the life of a tree is in its outermost and youngest ring,
    and not in the old wood of past years.
Like an aeroplane, religion must keep on moving or drop.
It is always bent on the higher things just ahead.

*O God, in the spirit of trust and humility*
*help us to go forward into each new day.*
*Speak to each of us the friendly and fatherly word that we need.*
*We are lonely without you.*
*Even our closest friend seems at times*
*far away and we wander alone,*
*a naked soul, in the vast solitude of the universe.*
*But you are our great companion.*
*We rest in you.*

# Taught What to See
## Luke 24:28-35

*Were not our hearts burning within us while he was talking to us on the road,*
*while he was opening the scriptures to us?*
(verse 32, Montgomery)

We see in the Bible
   what we have been taught to see there.
We drop out great sets of facts from our field of vision.
We read other things into the Bible which are not there....
If the Bible was not a living power before the Reformation,
   it was not because the Bible
      was chained up and forbidden, as we are told,
   but because their minds were chained
      by preconceived ideas,
      and when they read, they failed to read.

*You have set our feet on a quest*
*for the holy grail of truth*
*that out of that sacred cup*
*we may drink your life.*

# Dear Mother...I Have to Believe What Is True

*The next three reflections are from Walter Rauschenbusch's letter to his mother, September 24, 1886, responding to her concern about his unorthodox theology as he approached his ordination council examination.*

I have known it for a long time
that it would be more profitable
for me to hold the same beliefs as others.
But Christ says,
  "I have been born and have come into the world
  in order to give witness to the truth"—
that is, the truth and not the beliefs held by the pharisees.
For this he paid with his life.
And he also says,
  "He who is of the truth, hears my voice."
It is for me to ask,
  "What is the gospel of Jesus Christ?" and not,
  "What is the gospel of the people around me?"
I have to believe what is true,
and not what is held to be true by a certain class of people.

*Help us, O Christ, to realize that good people,*
*who desired to serve God,*
*crucified the Son of God for blasphemy.*
*Save us from their mistake.*

# Dear Mother…I Cannot Do Otherwise

When you say, "Stop worrying, believe in the entire Word!"—
   the same words came to all those who have brought us
   the purer truth we possess and who had to struggle for it.
If they had heeded this admonition,
   we would all today still be Catholics.
They would have had a pleasant life
   and would have lost their souls.
"To believe the entire Word?"
I have no desire more serious than to perceive
   and to believe the whole truth of Jesus Christ
   and the entire Word of God.
But where do I find this entire Word?
In the attitudes of the German Baptist preachers?
If this be true then we would have done no more
   than to exchange the infallible Roman Church
   for the infallible Baptist Church.
I don't know who could give me the guarantee
   that I was not turning my back at Jesus Christ and His teachings
   if I accepted, contrary to the urgings of my heart,
   the religious beliefs of this particular group.
It is daring what I am doing, but I cannot do otherwise.

*We pray for guidance on our path.*
*When we leave the plain paths*
*trodden by the feet of the multitudes*
*and strike off on the unmarked trails of the pioneer,*
*it is then we need you most,*
*and we pray for the clear shining of your sun in the day*
*and for a sight of some guiding star*
*when in the darkness of the night.*

# Dear Mother…I Am Stepping into Your Footsteps

As long as I believe that the voice of God
  and the word of God in the New Testament
  and also in the Old Testament are on my side,
I must stand by it, even though I may stand alone—
  but, thank God, I don't stand alone.
This is all the consolation I am able to offer you:
I believe in the gospel of Jesus Christ, with all my heart.
What this gospel is, everyone has to decide for themselves,
  in the face of their God.
I am now stepping into father's and your footsteps.
When you left the great and old Lutheran Church
  in order to join the small and ill-renowned Baptist Church,
you too invoked the right to interpret the Scriptures
  according to your own conscience;
    now, I am doing the same.

*O God, we thank you for those who have aroused us*
*to an active consciousness of you*
*and have summoned us again and again*
*to leave the outgrown home of the soul*
*for a larger mansion.*

# Tell God Your Pains

*This reflection is a portion of young Pastor Rauschenbusch's message for his first funeral in ministry—the funeral for a child held at the home of the Eisele family—during his first year as pastor of Second German Baptist Church, New York City.*

"Funeral of D. Eisele, child of Daniel Eisele," Feb. 24, 1887

Read Psalm 42

At such times as these the words of comfort and consolation rise very reluctantly to the lips. Any words a man can speak seem cold and feeble. They fall so far short of the reality of the sorrow.... We would best like to sit still with those who are stricken down, to let our hearts bend with them with the weight of grief and be silent. The love that unites us to the children whom God gives us is a most sweet bond. It is most like the love that God bears to us. There is no selfishness in it. We do not expect return of services we render them. On the contrary, the more helpless they are, the dearer they become to us. When we hold them in our arms, we feel as if something of our own freshness and innocence were restored to us. Ah, it is not easy to lose them. They are part of us, and part of our life is buried away when we lose them. And then the words of comfort are very feeble. There is comfort to know you have not lost your boy forever.... There is one who said with great tenderness, "Suffer the little children to come unto me, for such is the kingdom of heaven." And that same one has said, "Where I am, there shall my servants be also." If we are servants of the Lord Jesus, we shall one day be where he is and where your child is with him. Yet this does not satisfy you. You want him now. Your hearts cry out for him now. Your present loss is real, and nothing will undo it. But do take this thought to your heart that you will see your little one again and know him.... Dear friends, when you talk to God about the loss, you do not speak to one who cannot be touched with a feeling of your infirmities.... Tell God your pains. God alone fully understands you.

*O God, even if pain and sorrow come upon us,*
*grant us enough of faith to overcome the world*
*and still to rest in your peace.*

# Present Illness and Final Requests
## Psalm 116

*Precious in the sight of the LORD is the death of his faithful ones.*
(verse 15)

My Will is deposited with the Security Trust Co. of Rochester, which is Executor.

My important papers are in my safe deposit box at the Security Trust Co., and in my document box. Also in a drawer of my desk at home and in my office at the seminary. The vertical letter files on the left side of the big file and the portable files at home should be overhauled....

I want my old letters and personal things to be burned promptly without being read by my children, but the letters written me by the members of my family can be kept by each writer who so desires.

I do not want any of my lecture manuscripts, essays to be published, unless I myself prepare them for publication. My family can take anything they like; the rest should be destroyed.

My library (professional) should be distributed promptly to friends, or given to the Library of the German Department.

My family must decide about my personal scrapbooks, and other records of my literary work.

I direct that my body be cremated, as a matter of principle and cleanliness.

I leave it to my family and friends to arrange for any service, only asking for simplicity.

There are three hymns which have been especially dear to me, and on some occasion when convenient, I should like to have them sung for me.

I leave my love to those of my friends whose souls have never grown dark against me. I forgive the others and hate no man. For my many errors and weaknesses I hope to be forgiven by my fellows.

I have long prayed God not to let me be stranded in a lonesome and useless old age, and if this is the meaning of my present illness, I shall take it as a loving mercy of God toward his servant. Since 1914 the world is full of hate, and I can not expect to be happy again in my lifetime. I had hoped to write several books which have been in my mind, but doubtless others can do the work better. The only pang is to part from my loved ones and no longer to be able to stand by them and smooth their way. For the rest, I go gladly, for I have carried a heavy handicap for 30 years, and have worked hard.

—Walter Rauschenbusch
March 31, 1918

*Loving God,
if we at times feel the brushing
of the angel of death's robe,
or the summons of his touch,
grant that we may not fear
but trust,
through Jesus Christ our Lord.*

# Life Is Still Worth Living

*From a letter by Paul Rauschenbusch, written July 24, 1918, to his ill father, who died the following day, July 25, 1918, before the letter arrived.*

I look forward still, father,
   to our walking
      and talking
         and working together
some time in the not-so-distant future,
   when the world steadies to its keel again.
It has listed far to port for a time,
   but life is still worth living,
   and there's a better time ahead,
      when the off-shore gust has been safely weathered.

*You have cared for our outward wants,*
*and when we were full of anxieties for the morrow*
*and saw no way out, when the morrow came,*
*lo, you were still with us*
*like a pillar of cloud and fire in the desert,*
*and a way was smitten for us even through the deep.*

# Poems and Hymns for Life with God in Solitude

## The Hymns of the Church
### Psalm 100

*Come into his presence with singing.*
(verse 2)

The hymns of the Church
   are truly one of the best parts
      of her historical heritage,
   and one of the surest proofs
      of her spiritual value to humanity.
Our eyes must be hazy with prejudice
   if we do not love and prize
      the great expressions of personal salvation
      and religious experience
         which have been gleaned
            from all the vast poetical output of the generations
         and which constitute the common property
            of all religious bodies.

Rauschenbusch's spiritual life and faith were invigorated by hymns and their singing in worship, private and corporate. In 1890 and 1894, Pastor Rauschenbusch collaborated with gospel hymn writer Ira Sankey in the publication of two hymnals of gospel songs, combined in 1897 as "Evangeliums Leider, Nos 1 & 2." It is a collection of 344 hymns and gospel songs by, among others, Philip Bliss, Fanny Crosby, Robert Lowry, Charlotte Elliott, Frances Havergal, Annie Hawks, Harriet Beecher Stowe, Isaac Watts, and William Doane. Rauschenbusch and his German Baptist friends provided the German translations of all the hymns. He translated 134 of the hymns, including "I Need Thee Every Hour," "Rescue the Perishing," "Christ Arose," "Jesus Saves," "A Shelter in a Time of Storm," "All the Way My Savior Leads Me," "Showers of Blessing," "Marching to Zion," "Holy, Holy, Holy," "Near the Cross," "When I Survey the Wondrous Cross," and " Am I a Soldier of the Cross?" which was sung at his memorial service.

# "Jerusalem, the Golden"

## Bernard of Cluny

*A favorite Rauschenbusch poem/hymn.*

Jerusalem, the golden, with milk and honey blest—
The sight of it refreshes the weary and oppressed;
I know not, O I know not what joys await us there;
What radiancy of glory, what bliss beyond compare:
To sing the hymn unending with all the martyr throng,
Amidst the halls of Zion resounding full with song.

O sweet and blessed country, the home of God's elect!
O sweet and blessed country that eager hearts expect,
Where they who with the leader have conquered in the fight
Forever and forever are clad in robes of white:
In mercy, Jesus, bring us to that dear land of rest
Where sings the host of heaven your glorious name to bless.

The Christ is ever with them, the daylight is serene;
The pastures of the blessed are ever rich and green.
There is the throne of David, and there, from care released,
The shout of them that triumph, the song of them that feast.
To God enthroned in glory the Church's voices blend,
The Lamb forever blessed, the Light that knows no end.

Written by Bernard of Cluny, 1145, translated by J. M. Neale, 1851, *The Hymnbook* (Presbyterian Church in the United States, 1955), 238.

# "The Sands of Time Are Sinking"

## Anne R. Cousin

*Sung during the Rochester Theological Seminary memorial service for Walter Rauschenbusch, November 18, 1918.*

The sands of time are sinking,
The dawn of heaven breaks;
The summer morn I've sighed for,
The fair, sweet morn, awakes.
Dark, dark hath been the midnight,
But dayspring is at hand,
And glory, glory dwelleth
In Immanuel's land.

The King there, in His beauty,
Without a veil is seen;
It were a well-spent journey,
Though seven deaths lay between:
The Lamb, with His fair army,
Both on Mount Zion stand,
And glory, glory dwelleth
In Immanuel's land.

O Christ, He is the fountain,
The deep, sweet well of love;
The streams on earth I've tasted,
More deep I'll drink above;
There, to an ocean fullness,
His mercy doth expand,
And glory, glory dwelleth
In Immanuel's land.

With mercy and with judgment,
My web of time He wove;
And aye the dews of sorrow
Were lustred with His love;
I'll bless the hand that guided,
I'll bless the heart that planned,
When throned where glory dwelleth
In Immanuel's land.

The bride eyes not her garment,
But her dear bridegroom's face;
I will not gaze at glory,
But on my King of grace,
Not at the crown He giveth,
But on His pierced hand:
The Lamb is all the glory
Of Immanuel's land.

I've wrestled on toward heaven,
'Gainst storm and wind and tide;
Now, like a weary traveler
That leaneth on his guide,
Amid the shades of evening,
While sink life's lingering sand,
I hail the glory dawning
From Immanuel's land.

Written by Samuel Rutherford and Anne R. Cousin, 1857. See https://hymnary.org/text/the_sands_of_time_are_sinking.

# "Thanksgiving"

## Rabindranath Tagore

*A favorite poem included in one of Rauschenbusch's scrapbooks.*

Those who walk on the path of pride
   crushing the lowly life under their tread,
   spreading their footprints in blood
     upon the tender green of thy earth,
Let them rejoice, and thank thee, Lord,
   for the day is theirs.

But thou hast done well in leaving me with the humble
   whose doom it is to suffer
     and bear the burden of power,
and hide their faces and stifle in their sobs in the dark.

For every throb of their pain
   has pulsed in the secret depth of thy night,
and every insult has been gathered
   in thy great silence,
and the morrow is theirs.

O Sun, rise upon the bleeding hearts
   blossoming in flowers of the morning
and the torchlight revelry of pride
   perishing in its own ashes.

Rabindranath Tagore, "LXXXVI: Thanksgiving," in *Fruit Gathering*, first published in 1916. See the e-book by *Project Gutenberg*, released 2002, https://www.gutenberg.org/files/6522/6522-h/6522-h.htm.

# "My Country"

*Written by Rauschenbusch in his March 1880–June 14, 1881, poetry diary.*

My country, country of the free,
My heart in rapture swells to thee;
It yearns my weary head to rest
Upon thy great maternal breast,
Among thy valleys, hills and coves,
Thy glades, thy lakes, thy leafy groves.
To wander with a heart so light,
To breathe thy air, so pure and bright,
To search through all thy ample lands,
Where never yet reached human hands;
Ah, 'twould be ecstasy to feel
Thy freedom's thrill, and there to kneel
To Nature's God where yet she shows
The pureness, from his hand which flows.

—Walter Rauschenbusch
September 5, 1880

# "Still, Still with Thee"

## Harriet Beecher Stowe

*Sung during the funeral of Walter Rauschenbusch on July 27, 1918.*

Still, still with thee, when purple morning breaketh,
When the bird waketh, and the shadows flee;
Fairer than morning, lovelier than daylight,
Dawns the sweet consciousness, I am with thee.

Alone with thee amid the mystic shadows,
The solemn hush of nature newly born;
Alone with thee in breathless adoration,
In the calm dew and freshness of the morn.

Still, still to thee! as to each newborn morning
A fresh and solemn splendor still is giv'n,
So does this blessed consciousness, awaking,
Breathe each day nearness unto thee and heav'n.

When sinks the soul, subdued by toil, to slumber,
In closing eyes look up to thee in prayer;
Sweet the repose beneath thy wings o'ershading,
But sweeter still, to wake and find thee there.

So shall it be at last, in that bright morning,
When the soul waketh, and life's shadows flee;
O in that hour, fairer than daylight dawning,
Shall rise the glorious thought, I am with thee.

Harriet Beecher Stowe, 1855. See https://hymnary.org/text/still_still_with_thee_when_purple.

# Life with God in Service

# "Commit You All that Grieves You"

*"This hymn has been of unspeakable comfort to me. I used to sing my children to sleep with it. It is the best expression of that faith in the guidance and mercy of God which has sustained me in darkness and loneliness."*
(from Rauschenbusch's "Final Requests")

Commit you all that grieves you
And fills your heart with care
To Him whose might and glory
The starry skies declare.
He shows the winds their courses
And points the clouds their way;
Will He not guide your footsteps
And be your staff and stay?

The Lord must be your refuge
If you would feel secure;
His work must you consider
If yours is to endure.
No profit will it yield you
To pine in grief and care;
But God will lend His blessing
In answer to your prayer.

Your faithful love and mercy,
O Father, knows full well
The needs of all Your children
Who in Your shadow dwell.
And what Your wisdom chooses
Your might will surely do;
According to Your counsel
Will You Your work pursue.

Hope on, then, weak believer,
In trouble undismayed;
The gloomy night is waning,
Your fears shall be allayed.
Possess your soul in patience,
Be firm in God's employ,
And you in radiant beauty
Shall see the Sun of Joy.

This is one of the hymns the dying Rauschenbusch requested, written by Paul Gerhardt, 1656, and translated by Herman Brueckner (1866–1942), adapted. For original, see https://hymnary.org/text/commit_thou_all_that_grieves_thee.

# Inward and Outward
## James 1:22-25

*Become doers of the Word, and not merely hearers, deceiving yourselves.*
(verse 22, Montgomery)

I was born and brought up in a very religious family
   and was descended from a line of ministers,
     in fact I am the seventh in direct line of succession.
In my father's house I was brought up in a religious way
   and when I was about 16 or 17
     my religious experience began to come to me.
At this time it had no social expression in it.
I felt that I ought to do something for people but I didn't know how.
After a while I became a minister
   and my idea then was to save souls
     in the ordinarily accepted religious sense.
I had no idea of social questions.
Then I began to work in New York
   and there among the working people
     my social education began.
I began to understand the connection
   between religious and social questions.

*O God, we pray you to make us faithful followers.*

This and the following three reflections are from personal comments Rauschenbusch gave in January 1913, telling the genesis of *Christianity and the Social Crisis*.

# A New Feeling about Christ
## Ephesians 4:21-25

*You have learned to lay aside the old self, and to be made new in the spirit of your mind, and to put on the new self, created after God's likeness.*
(verses 22-24, Montgomery)

I wrote *Christianity and the Social Crisis* with a lot of fear and trembling.
  I expected that there would be a good deal of anger and resentment.
I left for a year's study in Germany right after it appeared
  so that I only heard the echoes of its reception.
I eagerly watched the first newspaper comments on it
  and to my great astonishment everybody was kind to it.
Only a few "damned" it.
The social movement got hold of me,
  just as the social awakening was getting hold of the country.
The book was taken…as an expression of what thousands were feeling.
People told me that it gave them a new experience of religion
  and a new feeling about Christ.

*Have mercy and patience with us,*
*and grant that our faulty and fragile work*
*may yet help to build what is enduring in your sight.*
*For though our hearts are dull and our courage faint,*
*we do love you, we do cleave to Jesus,*
*and we do desire the holy reign of God.*

# Urged to Give Up

## Mark 3:20-21, 31-32

*When his relatives heard of it, they came to take possession of him,
for they said, "He is out of his mind."*
(verse 21, Montgomery)

All this time my friends were urging me
  to give up this social work
    and devote myself to "Christian work."
Some of them felt grieved for me,
but I knew the work was Christ's work
  and I went ahead,
    although I had to set myself against
      all that I had previously been taught.
I had to go back to the Bible to find out
  whether I or my friends were right.
I had to revise my whole study of the Bible.
Then I began to write for newspapers.
That is where my ideas began to clear up.

*Suffer none to be utterly discouraged or to lose their way.*
*Suffer none to turn back and sit down*
  *by the camp-fires that are dead,*
    *surrendering the heroic call.*
*May we all realize at the outset that the way to God*
  *is a way of faith from beginning to end,*
*and that truth must be born amid sufferings and birth-pangs.*

# For the Lord Christ and the People
## 1 Peter 3:8-18

*Consecrate Christ in your hearts, as Lord.... It is better that you suffer for doing right,*
*if such is God's will, than for doing wrong.*
(verses 15, 17, Montgomery)

People didn't want to hear my message;
   they had no mind for it;
   they would take all I said about religion
     in the way they had been used to it,
   but they didn't want any of "this social stuff."
I kept on that way for eleven years in New York.
I lived among the common people all the time....
Then I came to the seminary and took up my work
   as a teacher of church history.
All this time I began to have a desire to write a book....
Most of the books I had in mind were scholarly books on church history
   which would have increased my standing as a scholar and a professor.
They were not dangerous books....
I decided, however, to write a book on social questions
   for the Lord Christ and the People.
This was a dangerous book....
It was part of my Christian ministry.

*We do not know what the days ahead may bring of joy and grief.*
*In all things we would submit to your will.*
*But whatever may come, suffer us*
*not to sink away into sin or a faithless life,*
*nor to bring shame on you*
*and on the holy cause to which you have called us.*

# Hold the Balance Even
## Luke 9:1-2

*He gave them power and authority and sent them out*
*to preach the kingdom of God,*
*and to heal the sick.*
(verse 2, Montgomery)

For my part, at least,
   I am a social reformer,
      though with feeble strength and sad cowardice.
I am also a Christian disciple,
   and in this double quality
      I have tried to hold the balance even.

*Grant us the proud joy of being co-workers with you,*
*children of God, siblings of humanity,*
*followers of Jesus Christ, instruments of the Holy Spirit,*
*builders of the kingdom of God.*

# The Heart of Jesus's Heart
## Matthew 5:1-12

*When he saw the crowds, he went up the mountain, and when he had seated himself,*
*his disciples came to him, and opening his lips he began to teach them.*
(verses 1-2, Montgomery)

Jesus has begun to talk to us as he did to his Galilean friends,
  and the better we know Jesus,
    the more social do his thoughts and aims become.
No comprehension of Jesus is even approximately true
  which fails to understand
    that the heart of his heart was religion.
No one is a follower of Jesus in the full sense
  who has not through him entered into the same life with God.
But on the other hand
  no one shares his life with God
    whose religion does not flow out,
      naturally and without effort,
  into all relations of one's life
    and reconstruct everything that it touches.
Whoever uncouples the religious and the social life
  has not understood Jesus.
Whoever sets any bounds
  for the reconstructive power of the religious life
    over the social relations and human institutions,
      to that extent denies the faith of the Master.

*O Christ, our Master,*
*our hearts go out to you*
*as we remember your life and passion.*
*Your every heartbeat was love*
*and all your desire was to help*
*the poor and heavy-laden.*

# A Fulcrum for God's Lever
## Isaiah 6:8

*Then I heard the voice of the LORD saying,
"Whom shall I send, and who will go for us?"*

When Archimedes discovered the laws of leverage,
    he…thought he could hoist
      the bulk of the earth from its grooves
  if only he had a standing place
    and a fulcrum for his lever.
God wants to turn humanity right side up,
    but needs a fulcrum.
Every saved soul is a fixed point
    on which God can rest his lever.
A divine world is ever pressing
      into this imperfect and sinful world,
    demanding admission and realization
      for its higher principles,
  and every inspired man and woman is a channel
    through which the spirit of God can enter humanity.

*Speak to us, Master,
and give us grace to hearken to your call.
Call us, and give us power to answer:
Here am I.*

# Jesus Took Her Side
## Mark 14:3-9

*They began upbraiding her, but Jesus said, "Let her alone. Why are you troubling her? She has done a beautiful thing to me."*
(verses 5-6, Montgomery)

When Mary of Bethany broke the alabaster jar of ointment,
   the disciples voiced the ordinary law of conduct:
      it was wasteful luxury; the money might have fed the poor.
Jesus took her side.
While the disciples were thinking
   of the positions they were to get
      when their master became king,
   her feminine intuition
      had seen the storm-cloud lowering over his head
      and had heard the mute cry for sympathy in his soul,
      and had given the best she had in the abandonment of love.
"This is a beautiful deed that she has done."
The instinct of love had been a truer guide of conduct
   than all machine-made rules of charity.

*We bless you for the human love
that has laid warm and tender arms about us,
cheering and comforting us.*

# Not Aristocratic Charity
## Matthew 14:13-21

*He saw a great multitude and felt compassion for them.*
(verse 14, Montgomery)

Jesus's love was not the aristocratic form of charity,
    but a working-class feeling of humanity.
He did not hand down packages of help,
    but met people on a level with himself.
The petition, "Give us this day our daily bread,"
    is not a millionaire's prayer;
    if a millionaire had devised the prayer
    I doubt whether he would have put that clause in it....
Those words, "Give us this day our daily bread,"
    come from a heart that knew human need and poverty.

*Be with us in the great things and the little.*
*Give us our daily bread and all things needful.*

## A New Avatar of Love
### 1 John 4:7-14

*No one has ever gazed on God; but if we love one another, God ever abides in us.*
*(verse 12, Montgomery)*

It is indeed love that we want,
  but it is socialized love.
Bless be the love that holds the cup of water to thirsty lips.
We can never do without the plain affection of one to another.
But
  what we most need today
  is not the love
    that will break its back
    drawing water for a growing factory town
    from a well that was meant to supply a village,
but
  a love so large and intelligent
    that it will persuade an ignorant people
      to build a system of waterworks up in the hills,
    and that will get after thoughtless farmers
      who contaminate the brooks with typhoid bacilli,
    and after the lumber concern
      that is denuding the watershed of its forests.
We want a new avatar of love.

*Help us to cheer the suffering by our sympathy,*
*to freshen the drooping by our hopefulness,*
*and to strengthen in all the wholesome sense of worth*
*and the joy of life.*

# The Prophets
## Isaiah 40:1-11

*A voice cries out.*
(verse 3)

The Hebrew prophets were
    the moving spirits in the religious progress of their nation;
    the creators, directly or indirectly, of its law,
        its historical and political literature, and its piety;
    those to whose personality and teaching Jesus felt most kinship;
    those who still kindle modern religious enthusiasm.
Most of us believe that their insight was divinely given
    and that the course they steered was set for them by the Captain of history.
Their writings are like channel-buoys anchored by God,
    and we shall do well to heed them
    now that the roar of an angry surf is in our ears.

*We thank you for the visions of glory*
*which your holy prophets have seen in ages past,*
*when their inward eye was unsealed,*
*and they saw the splendor of the Lord about them.*
*We thank you for the fervent testimony*
*which they have borne to your real presence.*

# Heartbeats become Pulse-Throbs
## Isaiah 40:12-26

*Have you not known? Have you not heard?*
*Has it not been told you from the beginning?*
*Have you not understood from the foundations of the earth?*
(verse 21)

The religion of the prophets was not
  the quiet devoutness of private religion.
They lived in the open air of national life.
Every heart-beat of their nation was registered
  in the pulse-throb of the prophets....
They looked open-eyed at the events about them
  and then turned to the inner voice of God
    to interpret what they saw.
They went to school with a living God
  who was then at work in his world,
    and not with a God who had acted long ago
      and put it down in a book.
They learned religion by the laboratory method
  of studying contemporary life.
Consequently their conception of God and of God's purposes
  was enlarged and clarified as their political horizon
    grew wider and clearer.

*We bless you for the prophets of God*
*who saw your kingdom from afar,*
*and caught visions of a higher truth,*
*and dared to speak it even though*
*they were despised and scorned for it.*

# Copying a Prophet
## Isaiah 40:27-31

*The Lord is the everlasting God, the Creator of the ends of the earth.*
*He does not faint or grow weary; his understanding is unsearchable.*
(verse 28)

No true prophet will copy a prophet.
Their garb,
   their mannerisms of language,
     the vehemence of their style,
  belong to their age and not to ours.
But if we believe in the divine mission
    and in the divine origin of the religion
    in which they were the chief factors,
  we cannot repudiate what was fundamental in their lives.
If you hold that religion
   is essentially ritual and sacramental,
   or that it is purely personal;
   or that God is on the side of the rich;
   or that social interest is likely to lead preachers astray;
  you must prove your case with your eye on the Hebrew prophets,
   and the burden of proof is with you.

*The cry of your servants has come before you.*
*Because they have loved holiness and righteousness,*
*they hated iniquity.*

# If the Prophets Lived Today
## Isaiah 1:10-17

*Remove the evil of your doings from my eyes;*
*cease to do evil, learn to do good;*
*seek justice, rescue the oppressed,*
*defend the orphan, plead for the widow.*
(verses 16-17)

The prophets were almost indifferent, if not contemptuous,
   about the ceremonial side of customary religion,
     but turned with passionate enthusiasm to moral righteousness
       as the true domain of religion.
Where would their interest lie if they lived today?
Their religious concern was not restricted
   to private religion and morality,
     but dealt preeminently with the social and political life of their nation.
Would they limit its range today?
Their sympathy was wholly and passionately
   with the poor and oppressed.
If they lived today, would they place the chief blame for poverty
   on the poor and give their admiration to the strong?
If they lived among the present symptoms
   of social and moral decay,
would they sing a lullaby or sound the reveille?

*Your servants raised their accusing voice*
*against the entrenched powers of vice and corruption,*
*and were sure that the voice of their anger*
*would be met by the thunder of your wrath.*

# The Worship God Demands
## Micah 6:6-8

*With what shall I come before the LORD?*
(verse 6)

Down the spiritual succession of Hebrew religious life
comes the proclamation that
there is one God
   to Whom all belong
   and Whom all must obey,
a God who demands as tribute and worship
   only one thing,
   namely, righteousness.
If you ask what that righteousness is
you learn that it is summed up in three propositions,
   to do justly,
   to exercise mercy,
   and to walk humbly before God.

*May the service of the Church*
*never become to us*
*a mere insidious form of worldliness.*
*Save us from the anxiety of faithless hearts*
*that know you not.*

# The Mountain was There
## Mark 1:14-15

*The time has come and the reign of God is near;*
*repent and believe this good news.*
(verse 15, Goodspeed)

The whole aim of Christ is embraced in the words
"the kingdom of God,"
    that this ideal is for this side of death,
      and not for the other side;
    that it is a social ideal
      and not an individualistic ideal;
and that in that ideal is embraced
    the sanctification of all life,
    the regeneration of humanity,
    and the reformation of all social institutions.
In the Alps I have seen the summit of some great mountain
    come out of the clouds in the early morn
    and stand revealed in blazing purity.
Its foot was still swathed in drifting mist,
    but I knew the mountain was there
    and my soul rejoiced in it.
So Christ's conception of the kingdom of God
    came to me as a new revelation.
Here was the idea and purpose
    that had dominated the mind of the Master himself.
All his teachings centered about it.
    His life was given to it.
    His death was suffered for it.
When you have seen that in the Gospels,
    you can never unsee it again.

*May we decide forever*
*that we shall not seek to build the kingdom of God*
*with the help of the devil,*
*nor trust his lying promise for success.*
*Grant us faith to trust you alone and your Spirit,*
*even when every step seems to be leading*
*to the failure of Calvary.*

# From Future Gaze to Here and Now Task

## Mark 4:26-29

*The seed is sprouting and growing tall.*
(verse 27, Montgomery)

Jesus rejected all violent means
    and thereby transferred the inevitable conflict
  from the field of battle
  to the antagonism
    of mind against mind,
    and of heart against lack of heart.
He postponed
  the divine catastrophe of judgment
    to the dim distance
  and put the emphasis on the growth
    of the new life that was now going on.
He thought less of changes made *en masse*,
    and more of the immediate transformation
  of single centers of influence and of social nuclei.
The Jewish hope became a human hope with universal scope.
The old intent gaze into the future
  was turned to faith in present realities and beginnings,
  and found its task here and now.

*O God, as we stand at the water-shed of a new beginning*
*whence we look backward over the past*
*and forward over the future,*
*we long to thank you for your mercies*
*and to commit ourselves anew*
*to your safekeeping.*

# The Kingdom Here and Now
## Mark 4:30-32

*How can we find any comparison to the reign of God,*
*or what figure can we use to describe it?*
*It is like a mustard seed.*
(verses 30-31, Goodspeed)

Because the individualistic conception of personal salvation
  has pushed out of sight the collective idea
of a kingdom of God on earth,
    Christians seek for the salvation of individuals
  and are comparatively indifferent to the spread of the Spirit of Christ
    in the political, industrial, social,
  scientific and artistic life of humanity,
  and have left these as the undisturbed possession
    of the spirit of the world.
Because the kingdom of God has been understood
  as a state to be inherited in a future life
    rather than as something to be realized here and now,
  therefore Christians have been contented
    with a low plane of life here and have postponed holiness to the future.
Because the kingdom of God has been confounded with the church,
  therefore the church has been regarded as an end instead of a means,
  and people have thought they were building up the kingdom
    when they were only cementing a strong church organization.
As we felt in our personal efforts
  the magnitude of the task of removing these evils,
  we determined to strike hands in the name of Christ,
  and by union to multiply our opportunities,
    increase our wisdom,
      and keep steadfast our courage.

*Give us the true unity between humility and courage,*
*and make us patient in our private wrongs,*
*but stern and outspoken when wrong is inflicted*
*on the helpless and the poor.*

# To This Task We Dedicate Our Lives
## Mark 10:28-31

*We have left our all and have followed you.*
(verse 28, Montgomery)

We desire to see the kingdom of God once more
the great object of Christian preaching;
the inspiration of Christian hymnology;
the foundation of systematic theology;
the enduring motive of evangelistic and missionary work;
the religious inspiration of social work
   and the social outcome of religious inspiration;
the object to which Christians surrender their life,
   and in that surrender save it to eternal life;
the common object in which all religious bodies
   find their unity;
the great synthesis in which the regeneration of the spirit,
   the enlightenment of the intellect, the development of the body,
   the reform of political life, the sanctification of industrial life,
   and all that concerns the redemption of humanity
   shall be embraced.
To this task, God helping us, we desire to dedicate our lives…
   and hasten with all our strength
   the time when the kingdom of the earth
   shall be the kingdom of the Christ.

*If our service is needed to help in the building of humanity,*
*may we rejoice that we have it in us to be of use,*
*and may we not repine even if we are weary.*

# For the Gospel to Have Power Over an Age
## Ephesians 6:13-20

*On your feet put the readiness the good news of peace brings.*
(verse 15, Goodspeed)

No individual, no Church, no age of history
  has ever comprehended the full scope
    of God's saving purposes in Jesus Christ....
It is on the face of it unlikely
  that the Gospel as commonly understood by us
    is the whole Gospel or a completely pure Gospel.
It is a lack of Christian humility to assume
  that our Gospel and *the Gospel* are identical....
The Gospel, to have power over an age,
  must be the highest expression
    of the moral and religious truths held by that age....
If the official wardens of the Gospel
    from selfish motives
    or from conservative veneration for old statements
  refuse to let the spirit of Christ
    flow into the larger vessels of thought and feeling
    which God himself has prepared for it,
  they are warned by finding people
    turn from their message as sapless and powerless....

*Save us from deceiving ourselves and others*
*with pretentious work,*
*with the turning of pretty phrases and thoughts,*
*while the majestic truths of God*
*stand afar off from our life*
*and we know them not.*
*Make us faithful.*

# Pulpit and Social Questions
## Luke 6:17-19

*He came down with them and took his stand on a level place.*
(verse 17, Goodspeed)

The ministry must apply the teaching functions of the pulpit
   to the pressing questions of public morality.
It must collectively learn
   not to speak without adequate information;
   not to charge individuals with guilt in which all society shares;
   not to be partial, and yet to be on the side of the lost;
   not to yield to political partisanship, but to deal
     with moral questions of public welfare
     which never do become political issues.
They must lift the social questions
   to a religious level by faith and spiritual insight.
The best time to preach on political questions
   is before they become political questions;
   before they have been thrown out into
     the general wrangle and snarl of politics;
   before they have become partisan matters.
After they become so, it is impossible not to become partisan
   in discussing them.
The Christian Church has the duty of treating questions
   before the world treats them.
Jesus said, "If your righteousness exceeds not
   the righteousness of the Scribes and Pharisees,
   you are not fit for the kingdom of God."
In the same way, I say, unless you see righteousness before the world sees it,
   you are not fit for the kingdom of God.

*Save us from spending ourselves*
*on little things*
*when great things*
*lie before us and cry out to us.*

# Church and Politics
## Luke 6:20-26

*Then raising his eyes upon his disciples Jesus began to say to them,
"Blessed are you.... Woe unto you...."*
(Montgomery)

Should a church ever exert its influence in politics?
We have a well-grounded dread
   of ecclesiastical influence in politics.
But that is due to the fact that, in the past,
   great churches have gone into politics to defend or acquire
      privileges for themselves.
It is an entirely different matter
   when the churches ask nothing for themselves,
      but demand protection for the moral safety of the people.
Then they are not one more selfish interest going into politics,
   but are the champions of the people and prophets of God.

*We cry to you and invoke your aid
in the battle of your people
against the powers
that blight and destroy.*

# Preachers, Pastors, and Prophets
## Luke 9:3-6

*They went forth, preaching the gospel and healing everywhere.*
(verse 6, Montgomery)

There are two great entities in human life,
—the human soul and the human race,—
and religion is to save both.
The soul is to seek righteousness and eternal life;
the human race is to seek righteousness and the kingdom of God.
The social preacher is apt to overlook the one.
But the evangelical preacher has long overlooked the other.
It is due to that protracted neglect
that we are now deluged by the social problem
in its present acute form....
A very protracted one-sidedness in preaching has to be balanced up,
and if some now go to the other extreme,
those who have created the situation
hardly have the right to cast the first stone.
The Church needs evangelists and pastors,
but it needs prophets too.

*O Lord, the anguished cry of your servants*
*has ever come before you,*
*when they have seen sin strong*
*and innocence broken*
*and trampled underfoot by wrong.*

# Flowerpot Religion
## Zechariah 8:16-18

*These are the things that you shall do.*
(verse 16)

We are often told that ministers
  who concern themselves in political and social questions
    are likely to lose their spiritual power and faith.
Professor George Adam Smith,
  in discussing the development of prophetic religion,
    says on the contrary:
    "Confine religion to the personal, it grows rancid, morbid.
      Wed it to patriotism, it lives in the open air, and its blood is pure."
I do not think so sweeping a generalization
  about purely private religion is just.
But those who hold that the flower of religion
  can be raised only in flowerpots
    will have to make their reckoning with the prophets of Israel....
All the world was God's field;
  all the affairs of the nation were the affairs of religion.
    Every great event in history
      taught the prophets a lesson in theology.

*We bless you that you are no hard task-master,*
*watching grimly the stint of work we bring you,*
*but the great master-worker*
*who labors more than all,*
*who leads our work*
*and rejoices with us*
*as we too learn to work in your great fields.*

# Modern Christianity Is Not Christian Enough
## Amos 5:12-15

*Seek good and not evil, that you may live.*
(verse 14)

We of "The Brotherhood of the Kingdom" believe
   in the spiritual life,
   in the fact of sin and corruption,
   in the need and possibility of salvation, in holiness and eternal life.
We have no desire
   to see evangelical Christianity bled to death;
   to see the church of Christ turned into a reform club;
   to see the hidden life of the believer toned down
      to a mild and sapless altruism;
   and to have Christian theology changed
      into a modern Gnosticism,
      into a system of evolutionary philosophy,
      with a place for Christ as one of the evolutionary forces.
On the contrary, we find fault with modern Christianity
   because it is not Christian enough.

*We beseech you to bless those*
*who may be plunged for a time*
*into doubt and distress of mind*
*when they find inherited traditions*
*that seemed so firm*
*breaking up under their feet.*
*Give them faith to go on as long as they feel*
*your hand upon them compelling them forward,*
*for in the end you will surely bring them out on firmer ground*
*and set their feet in the roomier spaces of a purer faith.*

# Protector of the Vulnerable
## Isaiah 42:1-4 and Matthew 12:15-21

*A bruised reed he will not break, and a dimly burning wick he will not quench.*
*(Isa 42:3; Matt 12:20)*

Is there a single situation in his life
   where Jesus came in contact with women
      that he did not stand up for them?
I do not know of any....
You remember when that woman "who was a sinner" anointed his feet,
   the fine gentlemen peered down at the woman
      and were contemptuously interested;
         but Jesus championed her.
When the woman was taken in adultery,
   he turned the situation and protected her.
When the grown people were trying to shoo the children away,
   and the apostles thought he was too busy
      to bother with the kids,
he insisted on having them in his arms.
When the children were shouting and hurrahing like the grown-ups,
   and the chief priests and the scribes were indignant,
he would not have them stopped.

*If anyone needs us,*
*make us ready to yield our help ungrudgingly,*
*unless higher duties claim us,*
*and may we rejoice that we have it in us*
*to be helpful to others as our neighbors.*

# Wealth Is Timid of Change
## Luke 16:14-15

*Now the Pharisees who loved money listened to all this and they jeered at him.*
(verse 14, Montgomery)

It is unchristian to regard human life
   as a mere instrument for the production of wealth.
The Church seeks to abolish things as they are
   and substitute things as they should be.
Wealth is the product of the world as it is.
Therefore wealth is timid of change,
   and its power has always been exerted
      to counteract
         and foil the Church
   when the Church
      has really been about
         its Master's business.

*Save us from squandering our opportunities*
*and then looking back at the end of our years*
*on a life that has been wasted*
*on doings harmful to us and to others.*
*Make us faithful.*

# Christmas and the Cross
## Luke 2:34-35

*Yea, and a sword shall pierce through your own soul also.*
(verse 35, Montgomery)

Christmas calls up smiling thoughts of love.
   We think of a babe nestling in its mother's breast,
     and of angels singing about "peace on earth and good will to men."
But Christmas began a life that was to end on the cross.
   That baby was destined to cry,
     "My God, my God, why hast Thou forsaken me?"
At Toynbee Hall in London,
   I saw a picture of the boy Jesus in his father's carpenter shop,
     gazing down at a cross-shaped shadow on the floor.
The shadow of the cross was over his life from the first,
   and because Mary loved him, she had to suffer with him.
Those who have helped to save humankind from sin
     have always had to suffer.
   "Out of the shadow of an agony cometh redemption."

*Your voice tells*
*of a message to be borne,*
*of suffering to be endured,*
*of a cross to be carried,*
*and our souls shrink and faint,*
*and we would fain have this cup pass from us.*

# Christmas and Purposeful Suffering
## 2 Corinthians 1:3-7

*Just as I have more than my share in the sufferings of the Christ,*
*so also through the Christ I have more than my share of comfort.*
(verse 5, Montgomery)

Because Mary loved him, she had to suffer with him.
Not all innocent suffering has power to save and help.
Millions of lives have been wasted in undeserved sufferings,
    and it is hard to see that their pain
        has wrought out any enduring good for humanity,
    except in so far as the sufferers themselves
    learned patience and courage through it.
The total amount of sin and suffering
    was not lessened by what they suffered.
It ought to be a great concern to all of us who suffer
      that our pain may serve others,
    so that those who come after us
    will be saved from what we have had to bear.
If our sorrows accomplish that,
    they have had a divine use and meaning,
        and are not a horrible riddle.

*O grant us in the hour of trial*
*the spiritual presence of our Lord*
*that like him we may say,*
*"Not my will but thine be done."*

# The Corruption of Christmas
## Luke 2:8-20

*Mary treasured up all those words, often pondering them in her heart.*
*And the shepherds returned glorifying and praising God*
*for all the things they had seen and heard.*
(verses 19-20, Montgomery)

The Church has a splendid obligation
   in regard to the holidays which she herself has created.
Christmas was meant for a day of holy joy.
The solicitations of our commerce have corrupted it
   and turned it into a time of frantic buying and selling,
   which drives all workers at terrible pressure.
Cannot the Church save the day from degradation
   and the people from cruel overwork?

*We beseech you that in these days*
*when all the world remembers*
*the lowly birth of Jesus,*
*he may be born once more in our lives*
*and may transform us by his presence.*

# A River Flowing from the Throne of God
## Revelation 22:1-2

*For the healing of the nations.*
(verse 2, Montgomery)

We of "The Brotherhood of the Kingdom" desire
  a completer surrender to the Spirit of God,
  a fuller life of trust,
  and a more ardent zeal for all missionary work,
  and for the universal reign of King Jesus.
But, on the other hand, we also believe in the social movement....
We refuse to regard it as a red-hot lava eruption
  from the crater of hell.
We hold that it is a river
  flowing from the throne of God,
  sent by the Ruler of history for the purification of the nations.
We see God's hand in it;
we see Christ's blood in it;
we see the creative energies of the Spirit in it,
  bringing out of its chaos the beauties of a new world.
But we must overhaul all the departments of our thought
  and work out that social Christianity
  which will be immeasurably more powerful
  and more valuable to the world
than either an unsocial Christianity or an unchristian socialism.

*Speak to our souls and bid us strive*
*for the coming of your kingdom of justice*
*when your merciful and saving will*
*shall be done on earth.*

# Divine Transformation of All Human Life
## 2 Corinthians 5:16-21

*The old state of things has passed away; there is a new state of things.*
(verse 17, Goodspeed)

When the kingdom of God dominated our landscape,
   the perspective shifted into a new alignment.
I felt a new security in my social impulses.
The spiritual authority of Jesus Christ
   would have been sufficient
      to offset the weight of all the [scholars]
   and I now knew that I had history on my side.
But in addition, I found that this
   new conception of the purpose of Christianity
      was strangely satisfying.
It responded to all the old
   and all the new elements of my religious life.
The saving of the lost, the teaching of the young,
the pastoral care of the poor and frail,
the quickening of starved intellects,
the study of the Bible, church union, political reform,
the reorganization of the industrial system, international peace,
   —it was all covered by the one aim of the reign of God on earth.
That idea is necessarily as big as humanity,
   for it means the divine transformation of all human life.

*May we not tithe mint, annis, and cummin,*
*and leave aside justice and faithfulness and mercy.*

# Character and Community Transformation
## Luke 13:20-21

*To what shall I liken the kingdom of God? It is like yeast.*
(Goodspeed)

Not only does individual opinion, in regard to anything,
   gradually bring about a transformation of society,
but when society is transformed,
   individual opinion is very rapidly transformed also....
I hold that it is the duty of all Christians
     and of the Christian Church also,
       to work in the first place towards the amelioration of personal character,
   and to have the influence from that emanate into society.
Certainly, that is true.
But we must not be blind to the other half of the truth.
We must also attack the wrongs of human society
     and the unjust laws of the community,
   to bring about righteousness through the kingdom of God in the world,
and then we shall also have an influence radiating from society
and centering upon the individual.

*Let us have such a vision*
*of the eternal and divine righteousness of God*
*that we can ever discern sin when we see it,*
*and ever hate it when we discern it.*

# The Great Thing
## Romans 14:15-18

*The kingdom of God is not a matter of eating and drinking,
but of righteousness and peace and joy in the Holy Spirit.*
(verse 17, Montgomery)

It is desirable that people acquire refined tastes and habits,
and these presuppose an abundant production of economic goods.
It is still more desirable that the goods produced be justly distributed.
But the main thing is not more goods,
   but more justice and equality;
     not a more luxurious life,
     but a saner, nobler life....
Jesus parted company with the social reformers of his day on this very point.
They wanted material prosperity.
   He did too, but he wanted first the kingdom of God and God's justice,
     and prosperity as the natural outcome of that;
       without that basis prosperity may be a curse.
It is true for nations as well as individuals,
   that the great thing is not the quantity or quality of meat and drink,
     but righteousness, peace, and joy in the Holy Spirit;
       that is, a just, peaceable, and glad life in the Holy Spirit....
Material improvements are important,
   but social reformers must not forget to look deeper than that.

*Give us grace to walk by the Spirit
which we have received.
May we pass from duty to duty
with tranquility of heart.*

# Has the Church Lost Its Saltiness?
## Matthew 5:13-14

*But if the salt loses its strength, how can it be made salt again?*
(verse 13, Goodspeed)

The Church still confines its ethics
 to the *personal* and *family life*....
The Church's message is still chiefly on the basis of individualism....
It is not strange...if humanity, amid the pressure of new problems,
 fails to be stirred and guided by statements of truth
  that were adequate to obsolete conditions....
The religious spirit runs surprisingly strong,
 but it runs largely outside the churches....
We are told that the Gospel has always met
 with indifference and hostility.
But is this today a persecution for righteousness' sake,
 so that Jesus would call us blessed for enduring it,
or is it a case where the salt is trodden under foot by people,
 because it has lost its saltiness?

*O Jesus, you have bidden us to rejoice*
*when others speak evil against us,*
*and to tremble if all speak well of us.*
*Grant that we may never be so wholly*
*of one mind with the world*
*that the world will altogether approve of us.*

# Teaching of the Church and the Ethics of Jesus
## Matthew 7:24-27

*Everyone who hears these words of mine...*
(verse 24, Montgomery)

In the teaching of the Church
　those elements of the ethics of Jesus
　which are in antagonism to commercial life
　　are toned down
　　or unconsciously dropped out of sight.
The Sermon on the Mount,
　in which Jesus clearly defines
　　the points of difference
　　between his ethics and the current morality,
　is always praised reverently,
　　but rarely taken seriously.
Its edge is either blunted by an alleviating exegesis,
　or it is asserted that it is intended for the millennium
　　and not for the present social life.

*Not only for the great ones of your Church do we magnify your name,*
*but for the little ones, the simple and humble folk*
*who did their day's work in obscurity,*
*and yet had your glory flooding about them.*
*Your love was in them, and so they learned to love.*
*The divine contagion of holiness went out from them*
*to bless the world.*

# Has the Church Had Its Day?
## Revelation 2:1-7

*Remember whence you have fallen, and turn again,*
*and do your first works.*
(verse 5, Montgomery)

Those who are trying to build up the new community institutions
   needed by our American life
      encounter the churches as a divisive force,
         bent mainly on their own prosperity and enlargement.
Those who are trying to arouse the working classes
   to a clear understanding of their interests and to solidarity of action,
      also find the Church blocking the way.
Granting that the Church has been useful in the past,
   is it not evidently failing now?
Has it not had its day,
   and is it not destined to pass away in modern life?
Is it not best for those who want to build the better society of the future
   simply to leave the Church to one side and travel their own road?
Such questions are in the minds of a great many people....
In fact, they are in the minds of many ministers and church members,
   and have acted as a partial paralysis of their enthusiasm.

*Forgive the shortcomings of our work.*
*Bless what was good, turn aside what was wrong and foolish.*
*Breathe through it all with your own life-giving and creative power*
*and bring your glory to shine amidst our weakness.*

# The Most Searching Test of the Church
## Revelation 2:8-11

*...that you may be tested...*
(verse 10, Montgomery)

The Church has been far more interested in the heavenly Christ
who came down from on high,
    was incarnated,
    died for us,
    ascended into heaven,
than in the human Jesus
    plodding on the dusty Galilean Road,
    the friend of all the world.
That is another cause of gratitude to the Bible.
Here in the gospels we find the Son of Man, the carpenter,
    who identified himself
    with the common people
    from whom he sprang.
The institution of the Christian Church
    grew out of his keen feeling for the social needs of the people.
He called the apostolate when he saw the leaderless multitude
    "as sheep without a shepherd."
If we inquire for the marks of the true Christian Church,
    the first and incomparably the most searching test is this,
whether it has lived up to the original intention and spirit of its Founder.

*You know our weakness*
*and if with worn body and weary hand*
*we still toil because we love you and your work,*
*your eye is upon us with love and joy.*

# Christianized Commerce or Commercialized Church?
## Revelation 2:12-16

*I have a few things against you.*
(verse 14, Montgomery)

If the Church cannot Christianize commerce,
   commerce will commercialize the Church.
When the churches buy and sell,
   they follow the usual methods and often drive hard bargains.
When they hire and dismiss their employees,
   they are coming more and more to use
      the methods of the labor market....
If the Church cannot bring business
   under Christ's law of solidarity and service,
      it will find his law not merely neglected in practice,
      but flouted in theory....
The law of the cross is superseded by the law of tooth and nail.

*Let us not be content, Master,*
*to tread the broad and easy path,*
*but make us willing and glad*
*to take up the cross and follow you*
*to the hill of loneliness and pain.*

# Make the Trial
## Revelation 2:18-29

*All the churches shall know that I am he
who searches the hearts and souls of people.*
(verse 23, Montgomery)

The Church must either condemn the world
   and seek to change it,
     or tolerate the world
     and conform to it.
   In the latter case
   the Church surrenders its holiness and its mission.
The other possibility has never yet been tried
   with full faith on a large scale.
All the leadings of God in contemporary history
   and all the promptings of Christ's spirit
     in our hearts
        urge us to make the trial.
On this choice is staked the future of the Church.

*You have called us to forsake the world
that we may know how to approach it;
to lose the world
that we may know how to possess it;
and to hate the world
that we may know how to love it.*

# Blemishes of the Body of Christ
## Revelation 3:1-6

*Call to mind what you have received and heard,*
*and hold to it, and repent.*
(verse 3, Montgomery)

As we exchanged our thoughts about the kingdom of our Master,
    our views grew more definite and more united.
We saw the Church of Christ divided by selfishness;
every denomination intent on its own progress,
    often at the expense of the progress of the kingdom;
churches and pastors absorbed in their own affairs
    and jealous of one another;
external forms of worship and church polity
    magnified and the spirit neglected;
the people estranged from the church
    and the church indifferent to the movements of the people;
aberrations from creeds severely censured,
    and aberrations from the Christian spirit of self-sacrifice tolerated.
As we contemplated these blemishes of the body of Christ,
    and sorrowed over them…, it grew clear to us
    that many of these evils have their root
    in the wrongful abandonment
    or the perversion of the great aim of Christ:
        the kingdom of God.

*Save us, we beseech you, from unconscious guilt.*

# The Church Has Not Kept Pace
## Revelation 3:7-13

*I have set before you an open door.*
(verse 8, Montgomery)

The powerlessness of the old evangelism
  is only the most striking and painful demonstration
  of the general state of the churches.
Its cause is not local nor temporary.
It does not lie in lack of hard work or of prayer or of keen anxiety.
It lies in the fact that modern life has gone through immense changes
  and the Church has not kept pace with it
    in developing the latent moral and spiritual resources of the Gospel
      which are needed by the new life.
It has most slighted that part of the Gospel which our times most need.
This attempt at a diagnosis of our ills
    is not offered in a spirit of condemnation,
  but of personal repentance and heart-searching.
  We all bear our share of guilt.
I have full faith in the future of the Christian Church.
A new season of power will come when we have put our sin from us.
  Our bitter need will drive us to repentance.
The prophetic spirit will awaken among us.
The tongues of fire will descend on [twenty-first] century men [and women],
  and give them great faith, joy and boldness,
    and then we shall hear the new evangel,
    and it will be the Old Gospel.

*O Christ, may we fight the good fight,*
*and hold fast the faith,*
*and walk even now*
*in the joy of our Lord.*

# Church and Money Power
## Revelation 3:14-22

*You keep saying, "I am rich, and have become wealthy, and have need of nothing,"*
*and do not know that you are the wretched one,*
*and pitiable and beggared and blind and naked.*
(verse 17, Montgomery)

I hold that the church and money power
  are not friends, but enemies,
    opposed to each other in the same sense
    in which God and the world are opposed to each other.
For the church is the incarnation
  of the Christ-spirit,
and accumulated wealth is the incarnation
  of the world-spirit.
The church stands for giving;
  wealth stands for taking, else how could it be wealthy?
The church stands for bending down to the weak and lifting them up;
  wealth, on the whole, stands for climbing up above the weak.
The church stands for sacrifice of self to others;
  wealth stands for the sacrifice of others to self.
Wealth—to use a homely illustration—
  is to a nation what manure is to a farmer.
If the farmer spreads it evenly over the soil, it will enrich the whole.
If he should leave it in heaps, the land will be impoverished
  and under the rich heaps the vegetation would be killed.

*Your spirit calls us to service.*
*We love our ease.*
*We love profit and honor;*
*we love the admiration and acclamations of people.*
*But you bid us to go out from our country and kindred*
*into the loneliness which you will show us.*

# The American Church in the Hour of Trial
## Philippians 2:5-11

*Let this mind be in you which was also in Christ Jesus.*
(verse 5, Montgomery)

We shall have to make people see things
    as Jesus Christ saw them,
  or as he would see them if he were walking among us today.
If we should leave political and social issues to be treated by others,
    we should infallibly lose the people....
My friends, let not the Church in America fail in this,
    its hour of trial.
The hour is coming for us, and the question will be
    whether we gloriously lead
    or ignominiously follow.
In case we should leave these things behind,
    it would bring disease into the life of the church....
    It would actually rot the church.
    It is now doing so.
Let the Church be faithful and say to the people,
    "We want nothing for ourselves;
    we are ready to give all for you."
Then we may safely assume a position of leadership
    in embodying the law of Christ
    in the laws of our country.

*May nothing that we buy or use*
*be stained by hardness or injustice.*
*Make our good-will intelligent.*

# The Church: Help or Hindrance?
## Galatians 6:7-10

*Let us not get tired of doing right.*
(verse 9, Goodspeed)

Is the Church an agency of social salvation at all,
   or is it a hindrance?
As soon as we step outside of the active membership of the churches,
   we encounter a large body of people
     who regard the Church without affection or enthusiasm,
       and in many this indifference rises by degrees
         to real dislike and anger.
Of course, it is possible for us
   to put up the shutters against this outside sentiment
     and still feel snug around our own fireside.
We can put it down as the sinful blindness of unregenerate people,
   or as ignorance....
But that does not account fully for the present feeling against the Church.
What ought to trouble us most
   is the fact that precisely those individuals and groups outside the Church
     who are themselves intelligently devoted
       to the redemption of our social life from its various evils,
         are in doubt whether the Church is more a help or a hindrance.

*May we not be anxious to perfect the externals of our churches*
*while the souls of people cry out thirsty for the living God*
*and none shows them where the living waters flow.*
*Make us faithful.*

# The Spirit of Jesus
## Ephesians 1:15-23

*God has placed all things under Christ's feet,*
*and placed him as Head over all in the church,*
*which is his body, the fullness of him who fills the universe.*
(verses 22-23, Montgomery)

I have tried to set forth the characteristic marks of the Spirit of Jesus, as they bear on the social task of the Christian Church:
   his indifference to ritual and speculative questions,
     and his insistence on righteousness and love among people;
   his compassion for suffering;
   his sense of solidarity with the common people;
   his faith in democracy and human equality;
   his fear of the spiritual influences of private wealth;
   his faith in human nature;
   his faith in love as a workable basis for human society;
   his critical scrutiny of all selfish aristocracies;
   his fighting temper;
   and his faith in the initiative of the individual who has faith.
If we will absorb from Jesus
   these fundamental points of view and impulses,
  we will be equipped with the most powerful motives of action
  and with the surest guidance in the moral questions confronting us.

*When we come to the determining choices of our life,*
*may we not seek after high things,*
*after fame and flattery,*
*after profit and ease,*
*but if need be,*
*may we follow him*
*who had nowhere to lay his head.*

# God's Pioneers are Always Few
## John 10:31-42

*We are not going to stone you for a good deed, but for blasphemy.*
(verse 33, Montgomery)

We all feel surer of our convictions
   when we find them held by great numbers
   and running far back into the past....
Only we must be very sure that we are really listening
   to the voice of God in history,
   and not to the unanimous consent of human sinfulness.
Majorities do not necessarily stand for truth and justice.
   They stand for customs and convictions of the past.
   They embody the solid experience and common sense of millions,
     but also their solid prejudices and superstitions....
God's pioneers are always few.
To trace the movements of God in history,
   we must not look to the broad bulk of humankind,
   but to the forward movements of those
   in whom the Spirit of God got a lodgment
   and worked the divine will.

*Make us strong in the Lord,*
*valiant in your battles,*
*ever ready to leap forward on your quest,*
*and if it may be,*
*let us see of the fruit of our prayers and efforts,*
*and be both sowers and reapers for our God.*

# The Church Is Where the Spirit Is
## John 20:19-22

*He breathed upon them and said, "Receive the Holy Spirit."*
(verse 22, Montgomery)

Someday a church historian may arise
  who will throw aside the traditions of that science…
  and write history on the principle:
*Ubi spiritus Christi; ibi ecclesia—*
  where the Spirit of Christ is, there is the church.
That historian will probably find the bulk of Christian history
  in the history of the heretical movements
  and will show how much social leaven was contained
  in all the reformatory movements of the church.

*O Lord, we lift our souls to you in the awe of the eventide.*
*Above the treetops hang the heavens in their glory,*
*but above the stars are you and the eternal silence.*
*We rejoice that in the quiet of your Sabbath day of rest*
*our spirits have been attuned to the melodies of your beauty.*
*We bless you for every word of solemn truth which has entered our hearts,*
*for every touch of loving hand that has comforted us,*
*for every opportunity we have had to speak some message*
*from our heart to the heart of our brothers and sisters.*
*We pray for your blessing on all who have come near to us this day,*
*on all who have brought us strength, on all who are sad and hungry for you,*
*on all your great humanity in its sin and beauty.*
*May our last waking thought*
*be a benediction on our fellows*
*and in our sleep*
*may we still be with you.*

# The Most Daring Faith
## Matthew 14:22-32

*"O little faith! What made you doubt?"*
*Then as they climbed into the boat, the wind grew weary.*
*(verses 31-32, Montgomery)*

When Jesus told his disciples,
   "You are the salt of the earth; you are the light of the world,"
  he expressed the consciousness of a great historic mission
    to the whole of humanity.
Yet it was a Nazarene carpenter
  speaking to a group of Galilean peasants and fishermen.
Under the circumstances at that time
  it was an utterance of the most daring faith—
    faith in himself,
    faith in them,
    faith in what he was putting into them,
    faith in faith.
Jesus failed and was crucified,
  first his body by his enemies,
  and then his spirit by his friends;
but that failure was so amazing a success
  that today it takes an effort on our part
  to realize that it required any faith on his part
    to inaugurate the kingdom of God
    and to send out his apostolate.

*We bless you for the apostles of the Christian faith*
*who carried the treasure of a new life in their hearts*
*and set their faces toward the dark places*
*to bless them with your light.*

# A New Apostolate in a New Harvest Time
## Matthew 14:14-21

*When Jesus landed he saw a great multitude, and felt compassion for them,*
*and healed their sick. "They need not go away," said Jesus,*
*"do you, yourselves, give them something to eat."*
(verses 14, 16, Montgomery)

Jesus saw the peasantry of Galilee
  following him about
    with their poverty and their diseases,
like shepherdless sheep
  that have been scattered
    and harried by beasts of prey,
  and his heart had compassion on them.
He felt that the harvest was ripe, but there were few to reap it….
If Jesus stood today amid our modern life,
  with that outlook on the condition of all humanity…
  and with the same heart of divine humanity beating in him,
he would create a new apostolate
  to meet the new needs
    in a new harvest-time of history.

*We bless you for the fellowship of your chosen,*
*for all the sons and daughters of the Spirit in past and present.*
*These are the true children of the promise,*
*the citizens of the heavenly Jerusalem,*
*the radiant points of light in the darkness of the world*
*for the revelation of whose glory creation waits.*

# Before We Pass Away

## Hebrews 13:20-21

*Now the God of peace…equip you in every good deed for the doing of his will.*
(Montgomery)

In a few years all our restless and angry hearts
   will be quiet in death,
but those who come after us
   will live in the world
     which our sins have blighted
     or which our love of right has redeemed.
Let us do our thinking on today's great questions,
   not with our eyes fixed on our bank account,
but with a wise outlook on the fields of the future
   and with the consciousness
   that the Spirit of the Eternal
     is seeking to distil from our lives
     some essence of righteousness
       before our lives pass away.

*Let us be of the number of those*
*who leave the world better for their presence,*
*that so when in distant days*
*those who come after us*
*continue their thanks for all the saints,*
*we too may be included in their thoughts*

# Poems and Hymns for Life with God in Service

## Hymns of Social Redemption
### Luke 1:46-55

*My soul doth magnify the Lord, My spirit exults in the God, who is my Savior...
who has put down princes from their thrones, and exulted those of low degree.*
(verses 46-47, 52, Montgomery)

Song must be catholic.
Whatever is nobly human has a right to be sung.
Every true religious emotion
   has a right to sing its own hymn,
   or at least to have someone else's hymn
   to serve as an aeroplane skyward.
Here is this big new enthusiasm for the salvation of social life
   and the dislodgement of ancient wrong. What of that?
Have we who work and pray over this
   till it becomes a physical pain,
   have we no right to a joint and adequate expression
of our feelings before God?
And what is more, have the working people,
   whose sufferings are more than sympathetic,
   not a right to hymns that will voice their own new hope
   and their heaven-born assertion of their worth and their rights?
If they prefer drums for the accompaniment,
   why, drums may rouse just as religious emotions
   as the *vox angelica* stop on the organ!
If the Church has old hymns of social redemption stored away,
   let us have them.
If not, let us make new ones.
But social redemption wants hymns.

# "God Save America"

## William G. Ballantine

*A favorite Rauschenbusch poem/hymn that Ballantine dedicated to "Dr. Walter Rauschenbusch, companion of travel and fellow-worker in the new social awakening."*

God save America, new world of glory,
New-born to freedom and knowledge and power,
Lifting the towers of her lightning-lit cities
Where the flood tides of humanity roar!

God save America! Here may all races
Mingle together as children of God,
Founding an empire on brotherly kindness,
Equal in liberty, made of one blood!

God save America! Brotherhood banish
Wail of the worker and curse of the crushed;
Joy break in songs from her jubilant millions,
Hailing the day when all discords are hushed!

God save America! Bearing the olive
Hers be the blessing the peacemakers prove,
Calling the nations to glad federation,
Leading the world in the triumph of love!

God save America! 'Mid all her splendors,
Save her from pride and from luxury;
Throne in her heart the unseen and eternal;
Right be her might and the truth make her free!

For "God Save America," see https://hymnary.org/text/god_save_america_new_world_of_glory. Also see William G. Ballantine, 1914, RTS Bulletin, *The Record*, 1918, 19.

# "Pikes Peak"
## Katharine Lee Bates

*A favorite Rauschenbusch poem/hymn text.*

O beautiful for spacious skies,
For amber waves of grain,
For purple mountain majesties
Above the fruited plain!
America! America!
God shed his grace on thee,
And crown thy good with brotherhood
From sea to shining sea!

O beautiful for pilgrim feet
Whose stern impassioned stress,
A thoroughfare for freedom beat
Across the wilderness!
America! America!
God mend thine every flaw,
Confirm thy soul in self-control,
Thy liberty is law!

O beautiful for heroes proved
In liberating strife,
What more than self their country love
And mercy more than life!
America! America!
May God thy gold refine
Till all success be nobleness,
And every gain divine!

O beautiful for patriot dream
That sees beyond the years,
Thine alabaster cities gleam
Undimmed by human tears!
America! America!
God shed his grace on thee,
And crown thy good with brotherhood
From sea to shining sea!

The poem was written by Katharine Lee Bates in 1893. Bates was a professor at Wellesley College and an admirer of Rauschenbusch. The original poem title was "Pikes Peak," and it was published in 1910 as the hymn "America the Beautiful." She revised her poem in 1904 and 1913. See https://hymnary.org/text/o_beautiful_for_spacious_skies.

# "God of the Nations, Near and Far"

## John Haynes Holmes

*A favorite Rauschenbusch hymn text.*

God of the nations, near and far,
Ruler of all mankind,
Bless thou thy peoples as they strive
The paths of peace to find.

The clash of arms still shakes the sky,
King battles still with king;
Wild through the frightened air of night
The bloody tocsins ring.

But clearer far the friendly speech
Of scientists and seers,
The wise debate of statesmen, and
The shouts of pioneers.

And stronger far the claspéd hands
Of labor's teeming throngs,
Who in a hundred tongues repeat
Their common creeds and songs.

From shore to shore the peoples call
In loud and sweet acclaim;
The gloom of land and sea is lit
With pentecostal flame.

O Father, from the curse of war
We pray thee give release;
And speed, O speed thy blesséd day
Of justice, love, and peace.

John Haynes Holmes, 1911, *The New Hymn and Tune Book* (Boston: American Unitarian Association, 1914). See also https://hymnary.org/text/god_of_the_nations_near_and_far?extended=true.

# "When Wilt Thou Save the People?"
## Ebenezer Elliott

*A favorite Rauschenbusch hymn text.*

When wilt thou save the people?
O God of mercy, when?
Not kings and lords, but nations!
Not thrones and crowns, but men!
Flowers of thy heart, O God, are they;
Let them not pass, like weeds, away,
Their heritage a sunless day,
God save the people!

Shall crime bring crime forever,
Strength aiding still the strong?
Is it thy will, O Father,
That man shall toil for wrong?
"No," say thy mountains; "No," thy skies;
"Man's clouded sun shall brightly rise,
And songs be heard instead of sighs."
God save the people!

When wilt thou save the people?
O God of mercy, when?
The people, Lord, the people,
Not thrones and crowns, but men!
God save the people; thine they are,
Thy children, as thy angels fair;
From vice, oppression, and despair,
God save the people!

Ebenezer Elliott (1781–1849), *Social Hymns of Brotherhood and Aspiration* (New York: A. S. Barnes & Company, 1914).

# A Responsive Prayer for All Who Labor

Almighty and merciful God, we beseech you to hear
the desire and prayers of our heart for all who labor.
For all who till the land and break the rocks,
For those in frequent peril of the sea,
For those in the dark and danger of the mines,
    We pray to you, O Lord.
For all who labor in factory, store, and office,
For all who work on the highways of commerce,
For all who teach and transmit the treasure of intelligence,
    We pray to you, O Lord.
For the women who toil of special danger,
For women who are bearing and rearing children,
For women who add the strain of labor to travail and motherhood,
    We pray to you, O Lord.
From child-labor, from ill-paid toil, from the drive of greed,
From overwork and fear of unemployment,
    Good Lord, deliver us all.
From toil without joy and hope,
From labor without pride and honor,
    Save us, O Lord.
That the oppressed may feel the salvations of freedom,
That the immigrant may live among us without suffering contempt,
That our commonwealth may be loyal to the higher law of justice,
That industry may join all workers in good will and kinship,
    We beseech you to hear us, O Lord.

—Walter Rauschenbusch, undated

# "They Will Say"
## Carl Sandburg

*Included in one of Rauschenbusch's scrapbooks.*

Of my city the worst that men will say is this:
You took little children away from the sun and the dew,
And the glimmers that played in the grass under the great sky,
And the reckless rain; you put them between walls
To work, broken and smothered, for bread and wages,
To eat dust in their throats and die empty-hearted
For a little handful of pay on a few Saturday nights.

Carl Sandburg, "They Will Say," *Chicago Poems* (New York: Henry Holt and Company, 1916).

# A Psalm of Great Cities

How wonderful are the cities that man has builded:
Their walls are compacted of heavy stone,
And their lofty towers rise above the tree-tops.
Rome, Jerusalem, Cairo, Damascus—
Venice, Constantinople, Moscow, Pekin—
London, New York, Berlin, Paris, Vienna—

These are the names of mighty enchantments:
They have called to the ends of the earth,
They have secretly summoned an host of servants.

They shine from far sitting beside great waters:
They are proudly enthroned upon high hills,
They spread out their splendor along the rivers.

Yet are they all the work of small patient fingers:
Their strength is in the hand of man,
He hath woven his flesh and blood into their glory.

The cities are scattered over the world like anthills:
Every one of them is full of trouble and toil,
And their makers run to and fro within them.

Abundance of riches is laid up in their storehouses:
Yet they are tormented with the fear of want,
The cry of the poor in their streets is exceeding bitter.

Their inhabitants are driven by blind perturbations:
They whirl sadly in the fever of haste
Seeking they know not what, they pursue it fiercely.

The air is heavy-laden with their breathing:
The sound of their coming and going is never still,
Even in the night I hear them whispering and crying.

Beside every anthill I behold a monster crouching:
This is the anthill of Death,
He thrusteth forth his tongue and the people perish.

O God of wisdom thou hast made the country:
Why hast thou suffered man to make the town?

Then God answered, Surely I am the maker of man:
And in the heart of man I have set the city.

—Walter Rauschenbusch, undated

# "O Love that Wilt Not Let Me Go"
## George Matheson

*Sung during the funeral of Walter Rauschenbusch, July 27, 1918.*

O Love that wilt not let me go,
I rest my weary soul in thee;
I give thee back the life I owe,
That in thine ocean depths its flow
May richer, fuller be.

O Light that followest all my way,
I yield my flickering torch to thee;
My heart restores its borrowed ray,
That in thy sunshine's blaze its day
May brighter, fairer be.

O Joy that sleekest me through pain,
I cannot close my heart to thee;
I trace the rainbow through the rain,
And feel the promise is not vain
That morn shall tearless be.

O Cross that liftest up my head,
I dare not ask to fly from thee;
I lay in dust life's glory dead,
And from the ground there blossoms red
Life that shall endless be.

George Matheson, 1881, *The Baptist Hymn Book* (Psalms and Hymns Trust, 1962), 20.

# Life with God in Solidarity

# "O God of Earth and Altar"
## G. K. Chesterton

*A favorite poem/hymn text of Walter Rauschenbusch.*

O God of earth and altar, bow down and hear our cry,
Our earthly rulers falter, our people drift and die;
The walls of gold entomb us, the swords of scorn divide,
Take not thy thunder from us, but take away our pride.

From all that terror teaches, from lies of tongue and pen,
From all the easy speeches that comfort cruel men,
From sale and profanation of honor and the sword,
From sleep and from damnation, deliver us, good Lord!

Tie in a living tether the prince and priest and thrall,
Bind all our lives together, smite us and save us all;
In ire and exultation aflame with faith, and free,
Lift up a living nation, a single sword to thee.

G. K. Chesterton, 1906, *The Hymnbook* (Presbyterian Church in the United States, 1955), 511.

# History and the Dominant Classes
## Hosea 12:2-8

*But as for you, return to your God,*
*hold fast to love and justice,*
*and wait continually for your God.*
(verse 6)

History has always been written
   from the point of view
      of the dominant classes
         and edited to suit their needs.
It has told about kings and priests,
   and left the common people
      under the gravecloth of oblivion.
It has erected monuments
   to the great destroyers of humankind,
   and stamped out the memory
      of the true leaders of the people
         whose wisdom might now offer us real guidance.

*We bless you for the martyrs*
*who stood firm in their faith*
*and feared not fire nor sword.*

# Speaking with Symbols
## Genesis 1:27, 31

*In the image of God...*

Human terms, when applied to God and our relations to God,
   are symbols and only symbols.
They approximate the real thing, but they are not identical with it....
So, we take human experiences and relations,
   enlarge them and make them do service
     to express God's relations to us.
But they are only symbols. Press them beyond a certain point
   and they become faulty and dangerous.
In speaking of the relations between God and mortals
   we must necessarily use terms
     borrowed from the relations between human beings.
Our language has no other symbols,
   nor is our mind capable of conceiving anything else.
"No man hath seen the Father."
"If ye see me, ye see the Father."
Whether we will or no, the only God
   we can think of or speak of,
     is a God with a human heart,
and the more we try to evade that necessity,
   the more abstract and vague and cold will our God be.

*Grant us, O God, to live a life with Christ,*
*and to enter at last, when our work is fully done,*
*into the rest which is reserved for the children of God,*
*and there join the throng of your elect*
*where your face is their sun and your love their light.*

# Speaking of Salvation
## Galatians 4:4-7

*So each of you is no longer a slave, but a child,*
*and if a child, then an heir, too, through God's grace.*
(verse 7, Montgomery)

Is it better to speak of salvation
   in terms borrowed from legal transactions,
     or in terms borrowed from the simpler relations of life
   in the family or in neighborly intercourse?
In building our theories of religion,
     should we build them on those expressions of the Bible
   describing the relations between parent and child
   or those describing God as a judge
     and mortals as condemned, pardoned, or justified criminals? …
In general, we may say that expressions taken from family life
   are preferable to those taken from court life.
For a judge does not love a prisoner, usually,
   while God does love us.
Hence conceptions of Salvation
   expressed in the language of the court room
   are apt to leave out
   one of the most important sides of God's character,
     God's love….
Expressions borrowed from family life are better than legal expressions,
   because in the family justice and love are blended and modify each other.

*O God, since we are all jointly guilty*
*of social conditions which breed disease,*
*may we stand by those who bear the burden of our common sin,*
*and set the united will of our community against the power*
*that slays the young and strong in the bloom of their life.*
*May disease that creeps from person to person*
*be a solemn reminder that we are all one family,*
*bound together in joy and sorrow, in life and death,*
*that we may cease from our selfish indifference*
*and together seek your kingdom and your righteousness*
*which bring us health and life.*

Rauschenbusch wrote this prayer in the midst of a tuberculosis epidemic.

# Whenever Jesus Looked
## Luke 13:1-17

*Jesus noticed her and called her to him, and said,*
*"Woman, you are free from your weakness."*
(verse 12, Montgomery)

Whenever Jesus looked at anyone singly,
   he saw and felt that person's divine worth;
    not on account of anything the person owned or knew,
   but on account of that person's humanity.
The child, the cripple, the harlot, were to Jesus
   something precious and holy,
   and he stood at bay over them when anyone
   tried to trample on them
    in the name of property, respectability, or religion.
He was always moving to break down
   the power of sin in the individual and of wrong in society,
   which corrupted or crushed this divine worth,
    and to furnish a faith, a spirit, a motive, and a human environment
     in which the lives of human beings could unfold in freedom and strength.
Whenever Jesus looked at people collectively,
   he saw and felt unity and solidarity.
   To him sin consists in that which divides,
    in war and hate, in pride and lies, in injustice and greed.
Salvation consists in drawing together in love, as children of one Father.
If any member of the human family is weak or perishing, it concerns all.
The solidarity of humankind was the great conviction
   underneath all the teachings of Jesus.

*As the sun goes down we clasp hands*
*with all the mystic circle of Christ's own*
*to feel the thrill of his power and of our fellowship.*
*Be with us through the night;*
*be with us through the day.*
*Be with us through time;*
*be with us into eternity,*
*through Jesus Christ our Lord.*

# Does It Draw People Together?
## Ephesians 1:7-10

*All things in heaven and earth alike should be gathered up in Christ.*
(verse 10, Montgomery)

Instead of a society resting on
   coercion, exploitation, and inequality,
Jesus desired to found a society resting on
   love, service, and equality.
These new principles were so much the essence
   of his character and of his view of life,
     that he lived them out spontaneously
     and taught them in everything that he touched
   in his conversations or public addresses.
God is a loving parent;
   people are neighbors,
    and sisters and brothers;
      let them act accordingly.
Let them love, and then life will be true and good.
Let them seek the kingdom, and all things would follow....
This would be Christ's test
   for any custom, law, or institution:
   does it draw people together or divide them?

*O God, you have bound our human race*
*in a great fellowship of service.*
*The work we have done this week*
*may serve the needs of people far away,*
*and we in turn are fed and clothed*
*by the toil of men and women whom we shall never see.*
*In you we all live and labor.*
*In you we are one.*

## God Looking at Us through the Eyes of Others
### Matthew 22:34-40

*Which is the greatest commandment in the law?*
(verse 36, Montgomery)

Jesus felt God looking at him
   through the eyes of his fellow human beings all the time....
He loved others;
   he really obeyed his own great commandment
   to "love your neighbor as yourself."
I think that principle was the direct product of his life.
Because he lived it he thought it.
His social life was the basis of his social teaching.
The fundamental thing for us to gain from Jesus is his Spirit.
Therefore his social feeling and consciousness
   is even more important than his social teaching.

*You have looked upon us*
*from the eyes of human beings.*
*You have breathed upon us*
*from modern movements.*
*But in the darkness and narrowness of our minds,*
*we knew you not and condemned you heedlessly.*

# The Sociable Jesus
## Matthew 11:19

*A friend of tax-gatherers and sinners!*
(Montgomery)

Jesus was very sociable.
He was always falling into conversation with people,
   sometimes in calm disregard of the laws of propriety.
When his disciples had returned to him
   at the well of Samaria,
     they were surprised to find him talking with a woman!
Society had agreed to ostracize certain classes....
Jesus refused to recognize such a partial negation of human society.
He accepted their invitations to dinner
   and invited himself to their houses,
     thereby incurring the sneer of the respectable
        as a friend of publicans and a glutton and wine-drinker.
He wanted people to live as neighbors and siblings
   and he set the example.

*As we go out among humanity to do our work,*
*touching the hands and lives of our fellows,*
*make us, we pray,*
*friends of all the world.*

# Our Business
## 2 Corinthians 13:14

*The grace of the Lord Jesus Christ, and the love of God,*
*and the fellowship of the Holy Spirit be with you all.*
(Montgomery)

Jesus seems to make love the test of everything.
In his description of the Great Judgment,
    the essential wrong
      with which he charged the people ranged on the left
        was that they lacked social feeling and solidarity.
They had allowed their fellow human beings
    to go hungry and unclothed.
They were unsocial.
He would test entire nations and entire religions by that same test.
Did you bind people together in love and justice,
or did you allow one class to prey on the other
    and leave the victims to their fate?
Jesus will not stand for any injustice or oppression.
He will not stand for exploitation or for indifference to suffering.
He will tolerate no religion and no economic system that countenances
    these.
It is our business to get that Spirit of Jesus glowing in us and all the world.

*Give us grace to win the hearts of wrong-doers*
*so that love may triumph over wrong.*

# Love Creates Fellowship
## Mark 2:1-12

*They removed the roof under which Jesus stood, and after making an opening,*
*they let down the mat on which the paralytic was lying.*
(verse 4, Montgomery)

The fundamental virtue in the ethics of Jesus was love,
   because love is the social-making quality.
Human life originates in love.
It is love that holds together the basal human organization, the family.
The physical expression of all love and friendship
   is the desire to get together and be together.
Love creates fellowship.
Love with Jesus was not
   a flickering and wayward emotion,
   but the highest and most steadfast energy
      of a will bent on creating fellowship.

*O God, Father of us all,*
*we praise you that you have bound humanity*
*in a great unity of life*
*so that each must lean on the strength of all,*
*and depend for comfort and safety*
*on the help and labor of one another*
*as sisters and brothers.*

# The Principle and Practice of Koinonia
## Romans 12:3-9

*So, many as we are, we form one body through union with Christ,*
*and we are individually parts of one another.*
(verse 5, Goodspeed)

One of the deepest principles of the New Testament
   is the principle of *koinonia*, of fellowship, of association.
One of the two ordinances of the Church is a meal of fellowship.
The early church made a bold attempt
     to realize this principle of fellowship in regard to property also,
   and the attempt has been repeated again and again
     in the face of overwhelming obstacles,
wherever a serious effort has been made
     to live according to Christ's law of life.
The power of association and cohesion
     was implanted by the Spirit of God;
   its theory was formulated by Paul
     in his illustration of the body and its members....
True Christianity emphasizes to the utmost the value of the individual
   and has been the real motive power
     back of the efforts to secure personal liberty.
But it contains more than individualism;
     it also contains the principle of association,
   and implants the trustworthiness, love, and unselfishness
     which cement people together
     and make association a workable idea.

*Lord Jesus, help us, we pray, to live your life joyfully,*
*and to give scope to your Spirit within us.*
*Make us women and men of God.*
*Grant that our life together*
*may realize something of the ideal of Christian fellowship.*
*May we feel the warm breath*
*of strong and noble bonds that unite us.*

# Putting Our Feet Under the Same Table
## Luke 14:7-14

*He told a parable to the guests when he noticed how they began choosing the best seats.*
*(verse 7, Montgomery)*

Social meals are often referred to in the gospels
  and furnished Jesus the illustrations for much of his teaching.
His meals with his disciples
  had been so important a matter in their life
  that they continued them after his death.
His manner in breaking the bread for them all
  had been so characteristic
    that they recognized him by it after his resurrection.
One of the two great ritual acts in the Church
  grew out of his last social meal with his friends.
If we have ever felt how it brings people together
    to put their feet under the same table,
  we shall realize that in the elements of Christ's life
    a new communal sociability was working its way
    and creating a happy human society,
  and Jesus refused to surrender so great an attainment
    to the ordinary laws of fasting (Mk. 2:18, 19).
Pride disrupts society.
  Love equalizes.
    Humility freely takes its place
      as a simple member of the community.

*May we enter into a fellowship of righteousness*
*to establish your law of love in all our land.*

# The Gregarious Nature of Humanity
## Ecclesiastes 4:9-12

*One will lift up the other.*
(verse 10)

The kingdom of God is a collective conception,
   involving the whole social life of humankind.
It is not a matter of saving human atoms,
   but of saving the social organism.
It is not a matter of getting individuals to heaven,
   but of transforming the life on earth
   into the harmony of heaven....
If Jesus put his trust in spiritual forces
   for the founding of a righteous society,
     it only proved his sagacity as a social-builder.
If he began his work with the smallest social nuclei,
   it proved his patience and skill.
Jesus never fell into the fundamental heresy of later theology;
   he never viewed the human individual
     apart from human society;
   he never forgot the gregarious nature of humanity.

*Enable us to give ourselves heroically for the good of all*
*because of our world's great need,*
*that by so doing*
*we may become leaders*
*in the armies of friendship.*

# Bound Together in Unity of Life
## Ephesians 4:1-6

*Make every effort to maintain the unity of the Spirit through the tie of peace.*
(verse 3, Goodspeed)

I believe in the miraculous power of the human personality.
A mind set free by God and energized by a great purpose
   is an incomputable force....
This power of the individual rests
   on the social cohesion of humankind.
Because we are bound together in unity of life,
   the good or the evil of one person's soul affects the rest.
The presence of one heart that loves humanity
   shames the selfish spirit in others
   and warms the germs of civic devotion in the chilly soil,
     so that they grow and bear seed in turn.
One brave soul rallies the timid
   and shakes the self-confidence of the prosperous.
One far-seeing person can wake
   the torpid imagination of a community
     so that others see the civic centers
       where they saw only real estate deals before.
Hopes and convictions that were dim and vague
   become concrete, beautiful, and compelling
     when they take shape in a life that lives them out.

*Grant us wisdom to deal justly and communally*
*with every man and woman whom we face*
*in the business of life.*

# The Goodness Jesus Seeks
## 2 Peter 1:3-8

*Become partners of the divine nature.*
(verse 4, Montgomery)

Jesus was not a Greek philosopher
   or Hindu pundit teaching the individual
      the way of emancipation from the world and its passion,
but a Hebrew prophet
   preparing people for the righteous social order.
The goodness which he sought to create in people
   was always the goodness that would enable them
to live rightly with their fellow human beings
   and to constitute a true social life.

*Since the comforts of our life are brought to us from afar,*
*and made by those whom we do not know nor see,*
*grant us organized intelligence and power*
*that we may send the command of our righteous will*
*along the channels of trade and industry,*
*and help to cleanse them of hardness and unfairness.*

# The Highest Type of Goodness
## Romans 15:1-7

*May God, from whom steadfastness and encouragement come,*
*give you harmony with one another, in following the example of Jesus Christ.*
(verse 5, Goodspeed)

All human goodness must be social goodness.
Human beings are fundamentally gregarious
   and their morality consists in being
   good members of their community.
A person is good when he or she is social;
   a person is immoral when he or she is anti-social.
The highest type of goodness is that
   which puts freely at the service of the community
     all that one is and can.
The highest type of badness is that
   which uses up the wealth
     and happiness
     and virtue of the community
       to please self.

*Enable us to submit, if need be,*
*the heart of fellowship to the spear of hate,*
*in imitation of him who,*
*renouncing ease and safety,*
*embraced the worst this world could do*
*that he might stand with the needy and lost*
*in their extremity.*

# Systemic Affinity of Christianity
## Romans 14:13-19

*Let us eagerly pursue the things that make for peace  
and the upbuilding of each other.*  
(verse 19, Montgomery)

There cannot really be any doubt
   that the spirit of Christianity
has more affinity for a social system based on
   solidarity and human kinship
than for one based on
   selfishness and mutual antagonism.
Democracy is not equivalent to Christianity,
   but in politics
democracy is the expression and method
of the Christian spirit.

*We pray, O God, for our dear country.  
May all its influence be for right and peace.  
As we speak for freedom and democracy abroad,  
may we enter into a new understanding of freedom at home,  
and wipe out the shame and wrongs of civilization among us.*

# Justice

## Amos 5:21-24

*Let justice roll down like waters,*
*and righteousness like an ever-flowing stream.*
(verse 24)

Justice is obedience to God's will;
the sternest words of the Old Testament prophets
   were directed against injustice
     and the oppression of the poor.
No sin except hypocrisy
   received so much attention in the teachings of Jesus.

*O God, may the time come*
*when we*
*need wear*
*and use*
*nothing that is wet in your sight*
*with human tears,*
*or cheapened by wearing down*
*the lives of the weak.*

# The Power of Public Opinion
## Proverbs 6:16-19

*There are six things that the Lord hates,*
*seven that are an abomination.*
(verse 16)

The ultimate power on which we stake our hope
  in our present political decay is
    the power of public opinion....
In reality this sheet anchor of our hope
  is as dependable as the wind that blows.
It takes strenuous effort to arouse the public.
Only spectacular evils are likely to impress it.
When it is aroused,
  it is easily turned against some side issue
  or some harmless scapegoat.
And, like all passions, it is very short-lived
  and sinks back to slumber quickly.
Despotic governments have always trusted in dilatory tactics,
  knowing well the somnolence of public opinion....
Now the justice and efficiency of democratic government
  depends on the intelligence and information of the citizens.
If they are purposefully misled by distorted information
  or by the suppression of important information,
    the larger jury before which all public causes have to be pleaded
      is tampered with, and the innermost life of our republic is in danger.

*O Christ, though Pilate knew you innocent,*
*and though he wielded the powers of Rome for justice,*
*he delivered you to death and shame,*
*because his life was evil and his heart afraid.*

# The Reign of Fear Is Never the Reign of God
## 1 John 4:13-21

*Fear does not exist in love;*
*but love, when it is perfect, drives out fear.*
(verse 18, Montgomery)

The moral instinct of people
   has always condemned competitive selfishness,
     just as it has always admired the moral beauty of teamwork.
Our hearts thrill when we see anyone throwing oneself
   heart and soul into a common task
   and risking personal safety
   to insure the common success.
By the same token we fail to thrill when anyone
   haggles for personal gain
   and seeks to get the better of others…
   and sacrifices social solidarity.…
We are taught to seek our own advantage,
   and then we wonder that there is so little public spirit.…
The reign of competition is a reign of fear.…
A reign of fear is never a reign of God.
Fear makes children lie and businesspersons cheat.
In competition the worst person sets the pace,
   and good people follow because they are afraid.…

*O God, if there is any duty from which we have been shrinking,*
*give us courage to clasp it to our heart*
*and make friends with our dread.*

# A Nation of Backsliders
## Luke 10:30-37

*The one who showed mercy.*
(verse 37, Montgomery)

In practice we are a nation of backsliders.
The whisper of awe and surprise
   that runs through the country
   when a powerful malefactor
   is actually brought to justice
   is proof that the rich and the poor
   are not equal before our courts.
The real decisions in politics are made by small cliques,
   and except in seasons of popular revolt
   the votes of great numbers of citizens
   count for almost nothing.
In actual practice the administration of public affairs
   is full of favoritism to the powerful,
   and even more full of damnable neglect
   for those things which are really vital to the common people.

*Almighty God, enable us in these trying days*
*to draw the deflected activity of our common life*
*into its true courses*
*by fighting those forces*
*which urge human beings to their ruin.*

# When Nations Die
## Psalm 82

*They have neither knowledge nor understanding,*
*they walk around in darkness;*
*all the foundations of the earth are shaken.*
(verse 5)

The simplest and most fundamental quality
  needed in the moral relations of people is justice.
We can gauge the ethical importance of justice
    by the sense of outrage
  with which we instinctively react against injustice.
If redress is denied us,
  we feel the foundations of the moral universe totter....
As justice
  is the condition of good will between individuals,
  so it is the foundation of the social order.
Any deep-seated injustice throws the foundation walls out of plumb.
If one class is manifestly exploiting another,
  there is no kinship between them....
If anyone can read history without the sickening sense
    of the enormous extent
    of injustice and oppression in all nations,
  that person has a mental make-up
    which I both envy and abhor.
Practically all internal upheavals recorded in history
    were caused by the agonized attempts of oppressed groups
      to resist or shake off the clutch of injustice.
Nations die of legalized injustice.

*O Lord, give us a day of salvation and rejoicing.*
*We know that there will always be sin,*
*and that it must needs be that offenses come,*
*but grant our mind faith and our right arm strength*
*to end the institutionalized wrong in our nation,*
*and give the young and the weak a living chance*
*to live a higher life,*
*and not to be destined from the outset*
*to ruin and despair.*

# The Abolition of Rank and Badges of Rank
## Matthew 20:20-28

*Not so shall it be among you.*
(verse 26, Montgomery)

Christ's ideal of society involved the abolition of rank
  and the extinction of those badges of rank
  in which former inequality was incrusted.
The only title to greatness was to be
  distinguished service at cost to self.
All this shows the keenest insight
  into the masked selfishness
    of those who hold power,
  and involves a revolutionary consciousness,
    emancipated from reverence for things as they are.

*We pray for humility toward others.*
*Save us from the sin of the Pharisee*
*who despised the publican,*
*though in your sight the publican*
*was the better man.*
*Save us from the cardinal sin*
*of the religious classes.*

# Unhorsing Privilege
## Philippians 2:1-4

*Let each of you in true humility consider the others  
to be of more account than yourself.*  
(verse 3, Montgomery)

Every successful revolution unhorses privilege
    and flings open the door of opportunity
        to some new group that has hitherto been shut out,
    and this has sometimes set free
        such an opulence of intellectual ability and moral power
    that all the damage and disorder of the revolution were cheap.
Injustice is the obverse side of privilege....
If anyone wants to promote righteousness,
    let them put a stop to privilege;
    and if they want to locate privilege,
        let them look for easy money.
The fundamental step toward Christianizing the social order
    is the establishment of social justice
    by the abolition of unjust privilege.
Logically this would be the first step;
    ethically it is the most important step;
        practically it is usually the last and hardest step.

*May we realize what advantages many of us have had  
over those who were raised  
under evil and oppressive surroundings,  
early polluted and loaded with the sins of others,  
that we may judge with your measure  
their brave struggles toward your light and holiness,  
and the half-heartedness of our own devotion.*

# Private Interest and Chronic Corruption
## Philippians 2:14-16

*In the midst of a crooked and perverse generation,*
*you shine like stars in a dark world,*
*holding out the message of life.*
(verses 15-16, Montgomery)

It is fair to say that back of every chronic corruption
   has been some private interest that needed silence or favors....
When private interests want something that is against the public interest,
   they are willing to pay for the favor....
Corruption in politics is simply the application
   of commercial methods and principles
      to the administration of government....
The most influential and permanent legislative body in the nation,
   the United States Senate,
      was notoriously under the control of the great Interests for years,
         and in many respects they turned a body
            that is to serve the common good into a force that betrayed it.
This is the essence of treason.
The Senators...in turn nominated the federal judges
   and fixed in the courts,
      which are now the most influential organizations of government,
   a number of judges who are constitutionally predisposed
   to side with the private interests against the common good.

*We pray you to end the reign of corruption and trickery*
*which has sold the birthright of the many*
*to gain the evil luxury of the few.*

# Class Chasm

## Philippians 3:4-7

*What was once gain to me, that I have counted loss for Christ.*
*(verse 7, Montgomery)*

Those classes which are in practical control of wealth and power
    have practically no reform program;
      they are anxious to maintain the present situation intact.
The middle classes,
    which share only partially in the advantages
      of the present social adjustments,
    have a list of grievances under which they chafe,
      but their social ideals do not differ very radically
        from the actual condition.
They want reforms on the basis of the present social order,
    and they can reasonably hope to secure them
      by peaceful and gradual methods.
But when we come to the disinherited classes,
    or to those nations which are forcibly held back
      from political liberty and social betterment,
    the chasm between their actual condition and their desire
      grows so wide that only a revolutionary lift
        can carry them across.

*Save us from the deadly poison of class-pride.*
*Grant that we may look all women and men in the face*
*with the eyes of a sibling.*

# Riches, Relations, and Renunciation
## Philippians 3:8-11

*In very truth I count all things but loss
compared to the excellence of the knowledge of Christ Jesus my Lord.*
(verse 8, Montgomery)

If the kingdom of God is the true human society,
  it is a fellowship of
    justice,
      equality,
        and love.
But it is hard
  to get riches with justice,
    to keep them with equality,
      and to spend them with love.
The kingdom of God means
  normal and wholesome human relations,
  and it is exceedingly hard for the rich
    to be in normal human relations to others,
    as many have discovered who have honestly tried.
It can be done only
  by an act of renunciation in some form.

*O God, grant that in the quiet of our life among kindred spirits
we may have foresight to decide
the leading questions of our future.
May we decide forever that we will not use your Spirit
to gain selfish ease for ourselves,
nor to arouse wonder by our display.*

# The Charm and Curse of Riches
## Philippians 4:10-20

*I know how to live humbly, and I also know how to bear prosperity.*
*I have been initiated into the secret of prosperity and want.*
(verse 12, Montgomery)

Jesus did not fear riches merely as a narcotic soul-poison.
In his desire to create a true human society
   he encountered riches as a prime divisive force in actual life.
It wedges society apart in horizontal strata
   between which real fellow-feeling is paralyzed.
It lifts individuals out
   of the wholesome dependence on their fellows
   and equally out of the full sense of responsibility to them.
That is the charm of riches and their curse.

> *Almighty God, make us to endure*
> *as good soldiers of him*
> *who as a babe lay helpless on a maiden's breast*
> *and as a man hung helpless on a wooden cross,*
> *Jesus Christ, your Son, our Savior.*
> *Write deep into our hearts*
> *the pain and suffering.*

# Economics and Politics
## James 5:1-6

*The cries of the harvesters*
*have reached the ears of the Lord of Hosts.*
(verse 4, Goodspeed)

Any shifting of the economic equilibrium
   from one class to another
is sure to be followed by a shifting
   of the political equilibrium.
If a class arrives at economic wealth,
   it will gain political influence
   and some form of representation....
A class which is economically strong
   will have the necessary influence
   to secure and enforce laws
   which protect its economic interests.
In turn, a class which controls legislation
   will shape it for its own enrichment.
Politics is embroidered with patriotic sentiment and phrases,
   but at bottom, consciously or unconsciously,
     the economic interests dominate it always.

*O God, your call calls us away from sin;*
*it summons us to holiness of life;*
*and all our soul assents to its commands,*
*and yet all our life rebels against it.*

# An Outrageous Betrayal of Justice
## Isaiah 59:12-15

*Justice is turned back,*
*and righteousness stands at a distance,*
*for truth stumbles in the public square,*
*and uprightness cannot enter.*
*Truth is lacking,*
*and whoever turns from evil is despoiled.*
(verses 14-15)

When the rich and the poor
   have justice meted to them in our courts
      with an uneven hand,
      and the act is made plain and comprehensible,
   it is felt to be an outrage
   and a betrayal of the spirit of our institutions.
When powerful interests receive special consideration
   and benefits from Congress or the State legislatures,
      all concerned are careful to mask the fact
      and disguise the action
      as if it were done for the public interest.
When the property of the rich is partly exempted
   from taxation by unequal methods of assessments,
   and the burden of public expenditure
      is thrown on the poorer classes,
   we feel free to protest against it as a departure
   from the clear intent of our fundamental laws.
In short, inequality and oppression,
   the denial of equal rights
   and of the equal humanity of all
   is felt to be a backsliding and disgrace.

*O God, may we not unknowingly inflict suffering*
*through selfish indifference*
*or the willful ignorance of a callous heart.*

# A *De Facto* Emperor

## Ephesians 6:10-12

*Our wrestling is against despotism, the empires, the rulers of this present darkness.*
(verse 12, Montgomery)

We have, in fact, one kind of constitution on paper,
    and another system of government in fact.
That is usually the way when a slow revolution is taking place
    in the distribution of political and economic power.
The old structure apparently remains intact,
    but actually the seat of power has changed....
The president of a great university has predicted
    that we shall have an emperor within twenty years.
We shall probably never have an emperor,
    but we may have...some person not even mentioned
        in the constitution or law,
        who will be the *de facto* emperor of our republic.
    Names are trifles. An emperor by any other name will smell as sweet....
The boss in American political life
    is the extra-constitutional ruler
        simply because he stands for the really dominant powers.

*O Lord, in a few days more, with the election,*
*the future of our country will once more*
*have received an impress that will last,*
*and will bring further effects after it.*
*We pray to you for success wherever the people strive*
*to regain their freedom and self-government*
*from the irresponsible powers that have usurped them.*

# Forgive and Repair Torn Tissues

## Matthew 5:23, 24, 38-42; 18:21, 22

*Go and make friends with your brother or sister, first of all;*
*then come and offer your gift.*
(verse 24, Montgomery)

The force of love's unitive will
  is best seen where fellowship is in danger of disruption.
If someone has offended us,
    that fact is not to break up our kinship,
  but we must forgive and forgive and forgive,
    and always stand ready
    to repair the torn tissues of fellowship.
If we remember that we have offended
    and our brother or sister is now alienated from us,
  we are to drop everything…and go and recreate fellowship.
If someone hates us or persecutes and reviles us,
    we must refuse to let kinship be ruined,
  and must woo the sibling back with love and blessings.
If someone smites us in the face,
    we must turn the other cheek
    instead of doubling the barrier by returning the blow.
These are simply the most empathic expressions
   of the determination that the familial relation
     which binds us together
  must not be ruptured.

*O God, give us a forgiving heart.*
*Let not your Holy Spirit suffer us to cherish*
*the dark thoughts of resentment and revenge.*
*Even when we are wronged, and our wrong burns,*
*may we still love those who hurt us,*
*because they are human, sinful and erring like ourselves.*
*If we remember that our brother or sister is now*
*sore and stricken because we have wronged them,*
*give us a swift responsiveness to the persuading love of Christ,*
*that we may seek them out and confess our wrong,*
*and so re-establish the broken fellowship.*

# The Real Zest of Life
## 2 Corinthians 3:17-18

*Where the Spirit of the Lord abides there is freedom.*
(verse 17, Montgomery)

Only those who have lived where liberty is scarce know its sweetness.
As a young man I spent four years in Germany.
On my return to my native country, I was conscious,
   not only of the thrill of a young patriot,
     but also of an invigorating ease and freedom in dealing with people.
I studied the cause of the sensation
   and concluded that it was due to the larger freedom
     accorded here by everybody to everybody....
Freedom gives the real zest to life.
Freedom is also necessary to develop a nation of vigorous characters.
A high level of culture and ability can be produced without freedom....
But it will be the commonplace usefulness of barnyard fowl,
   assiduously laying eggs, but without wing enough to fly over the fence.
If socialism takes away our freedom,
   it stifles the future leaders of humanity before their birth.
On the other hand it is well for the advocates of personal liberty,
   who urge this objection against socialism,
     to remember that liberty is today the possession of a favored few.

*O God, we rejoice in the growing freedom of your life within us.*
*There was a time when we were bondservants*
*and did your will under compulsion*
*from fear of punishment in time and eternity.*
*But you have made us children of God*
*through your first-born son, Jesus Christ, our elder brother.*

# The Pronunciamento and Platform of Christianity
## Luke 4:11-21

*This passage of scripture has been fulfilled here in your hearing today.*
(verse 21, Goodspeed)

*The Spirit of the Lord Jehovah is upon me,*
*Because Jehovah hath anointed me to proclaim glad tidings to the poor;*
*He hath sent me to bind up the broken hearted;*
*To proclaim liberty to the captives*
*And the bursting of the prison to them that are bound;*
*To proclaim the year of Jehovah's favor,*
*And the day of vengeance of our God.*
Jesus declared that he found the purpose of his own mission
    in fulfilling this Isaiah prophecy,
    and thereby he adopted it
    as the pronunciamento and platform of Christianity.
The words reverberate with freedom,
    and whenever the Gospel has retained
    even a breath of the Spirit of Jesus in it,
    it has been a force making for freedom.
Christianity necessarily must be on the side of freedom
    if it is to fulfill its twofold purpose
    of creating strong and saved characters,
    and of establishing a redeemed and communal social life....
Human beings have no communal relations
    until they face one another
with a sense of freedom and of equal humanity.

*We are not content to save our souls.*
*We want a share in your great work of redemption.*
*We want to dry the tears of those who weep,*
*to cheer those who walk in the darkness,*
*to strengthen those who are sinking away into temptation and sin,*
*to break the yoke of the oppressed,*
*to stop the hands of those who unconsciously*
*are bruising and killing human life.*

# The Barrier Is Still Broad
## Romans 12:9-13

*Practice hospitality to strangers.*
(verse 13, Montgomery)

The sense of humanity works horizontally sideways,
   as well as perpendicularly downwards.
It quickens the feeling of interest and kinship
   between nations and races.
The student of history knows what barriers
   the difference of nationality and religion
   has drawn between people in the past.
In Latin the word for stranger
   and the word for enemy were the same.
The barrier is still broad.

*O God, as in the days of our sins*
*we have drawn others down with us,*
*help us now to draw others up with us to God.*

# Open to All Who Will Come In
## Romans 12:14-18

*Aim to do what is honorable in the eyes of all.*
(verse 17, Montgomery)

I do not believe it is right to restrict immigration....
I think also if any one of you were living at a minor seaport
  or some little town on the coast,
    and a little vessel landed out there
      with a few immigrants trying to come in,
    I think very few of you would be willing to let them in....
I believe in throwing open this country to all who will come in,
  for I believe God made it for all.
Who are we that we should close this country
  against the rest of the world?
We all came over here sometime;
  if we did not, our parents or our grandparents
    were all immigrants at one time.
Think of a vessel being wrecked;
  the life-saving crew goes out to rescue them
    and takes in enough into the boat to fill up the benches comfortably,
  while there are plenty of other wretches out in the water
    eager to be saved;
  suppose those in the boat should say to those outside,
    we cannot take you in, it would inconvenience us,
  and if the poor wretches got their hands on the gunwale,
    the others would drive them into the waters,
  would it not be driving them back into a living death?
We are driving people back into poverty.
Let all the nations come in. Throw open the resources of this country.
Let them go to work with the chances they have
  and there will be plenty of opportunities to gain the bread they wish.
I think this very pressure of population
  brought on by immigration is a boon to us.

> *O Master, we rejoice in Paul's large mind and flaming soul,*
>   *in the far-sighted wisdom of his plans,*
>     *in the unconquerable faith that stayed him*
> *in the midst of physical suffering and persecution and loneliness,*
>   *for the wholeness of his devotion that counted not his life dear*
> *if only he could fulfil the ministry which he had received from you.*

# The Nerve of the Social Movement
## Romans 13:8-10

*Never owe anyone anything save the debt of love.*
(verse 8, Montgomery)

The starting point of the social movement
   is the conviction of the inherent worth of a human being.
Its goal is to secure the recognition of that worth
   in all departments of life....
That sentiment is the nerve of the social movement;
   the rest is muscle.
If that nerve were dead or paralyzed
   there would be no social movement....
Now that sentiment seeks embodiment.
It seeks to stop that which offends it;
   it seeks to create conditions which it can accept....
Here then we have a great movement
   actuated by the conviction that a human life is precious,
   and seeking to give every person
     an opportunity to live one's life worthily.

*O God, we invoke your blessing on all the men and women*
*who have toiled to build and warm our homes,*
*to fashion our raiment,*
*and to wrest from sea and land the food*
*that nourishes us and our children.*
*We pray that they may have health and joy,*
*and hope and love, even as we desire for own loved ones.*

# Shoulder to Shoulder
## Psalm 133

*How good and pleasant it is
when kindred live together in unity!*
(verse 1)

Christian union is best achieved,
   not by doctrinal discussions,
   nor by formal resolutions of unity,
but by working shoulder to shoulder
   with those of other churches
and realizing the living Christ
   who shines from their eyes
   and speaks with their lips.
We cannot well hate our team-mates
   who have stood by us in hard fights.

*O God, if others speak well of us,
may we not be puffed up,
and if they slight us, may we not be cast down.
Teach us to take heed to all the judgments of others
and to gather patiently whatever truth there may be in them,
but ever to look upward to see if human judgment
receives its ratification from the only one who is our Master,
even Christ.*

# One Torch Kindling Hundreds
## Matthew 5:14-16

*Let your light shine before others that they may see the good you do,*
*and give glory to your Father who is in heaven.*
(verse 16, Montgomery)

No torch is kindled of itself,
   but when one person has lighted a torch at the altar of God,
   hundreds will take their light from that one torch.
So the faith of the pioneers becomes socialized.
The belief of the few
   in time
  becomes a dogma
   which does not have to be proved over and over,
     but is a spiritual fund owned in common
     by a great social group.
We need new dogmas that will raise
   the old to a new level and give them wider scope.
"You have heard that it was said of old time—
   but I say unto you."
Such a lifting of moral conviction comes through those
   who can speak with authority
   because they speak for God.

*O God, bless the work of this day.*
*Forgive our sloth and our petty zeal,*
*our ambition and our lack of it,*
*and use all our faltering human efforts*
*and all these fragmentary days*
*to do your work in and through us,*
*so that the glory of the Lord may shine brightly within us*
*and we may even now live the life eternal.*

# Let Us Counsel Patience
## James 5:7-11

*Behold the farmer who waits for the precious fruit of the earth,*
*being patient over it, until it gets the early and the latter rains.*
(verse 7, Montgomery)

The slow conflict of opposing forces
  is God's method of educating a nation....
In the peaceful conflict
  crude schemes are melted down and refined;
  ideas are elaborated;
  the public mind is permeated;
  old fogies die;
  a young generation grows up
    with the new ideals bred in their bones;
  and when the change comes, it has a backing in the people.
While if it were forced on an indifferent or hostile majority
    by a determined minority,
  there would be a reaction, a repeal,
    and a great and wise measure
      would go down to the record of posterity
        discredited and abolished after trial.
Therefore let us counsel patience,
  not for the sake of the people
    who might get hurt in a scrimmage,
  but for the sake of the cause and its ultimate success.

*Bless the day's work that is drawing to an end.*
*Our life seems but feeble and its accomplishments small,*
*but if it is centered in you, it will be great in the end.*
*All our actions then will not be like scattered rubbish,*
*but like stones, laid one by one*
*above the cornerstone of a great purpose,*
*and building upon a habitation of God in the Spirit.*

# The Process Is Never Complete
## Jude 24-25

*As it was before time began, is now,*
*and ever shall be to all the ages.*
(verse 25, Montgomery)

Human nature is the raw material for the Christian character.
The Spirit of Christ working in the human spirit is to
   elevate the aims,
   ennoble the motives,
   and intensify the affections.
This process is never complete.
The Christian is always but in the making.
In the same way human society
   is the raw material for the Christian society.
The Spirit of Christ is to hallow all the natural relations of humanity
   and give them a divine significance and value.
This process, too, is never complete.
The kingdom of God is always but coming.

*O God, we come before you*
*as a company of those whom you*
*have called into your service....*
*We face an unknown future.*
*We know that your kingdom is to be established*
*and that we are to have some part in it,*
*but we are borne down by the sense of our helplessness*
*and are pressed by the unsolved questions that face us.*

# No Smooth Road

## Mark 8:31-38

*If any wish to follow me, let them renounce self,*
*take up their cross, and so follow me.*
(verse 34, Montgomery)

The coming of the kingdom of God
  will not be by peaceful development only,
  but by conflict with the kingdom of Evil.
We should estimate the power of sin too lightly
  if we forecast a smooth road.
The cross of Christ put God's approval
  on the sacrificial impulse in the hearts of the brave....
It has set them free from the fear of pain
    and the fear of others,
  and given them a certain finishing quality of strength.
It has inspired courage and defiance of evil....
The death of Jesus was the clearest
  and most conspicuous case of prophetic suffering....
His death comforted and supported
  all who bore prophetic suffering
  by the consciousness that they
  were "bearing the marks of the Lord Jesus"
  and were carrying on what he had borne.

*Our Master, by the loneliness of your loving life,*
*by the shame of your sufferings,*
*by the agony of our loving cries upon the cross,*
*we vow anew to take our cross upon us and follow you*
*and to carry forward the great mission*
*for which your life was spent and your blood was shed.*

# A Solidarity of Hate and Horror
## Psalm 33:16-22

*The war horse is a vain hope for victory,*
*and by its great might it can not save.*
*(verse 17)*

In some of our swampy forests the growth of ages
   has produced impenetrable thickets of trees and undergrowth,
  woven together by creepers,
   and inhabited by things that creep or fly.
Every season sends forth new growth under the urge of life,
  but always developing from the old growth and its seeds,
   and still perpetuating the same rank mass of life.
The life of humanity is infinitely interwoven,
  always renewing itself,
   yet always perpetuating what has been.
The evils of one generation
  are caused by the wrongs of the generations that preceded,
  and will in turn condition the sufferings and temptations
   of those who come after....
One nation arms because it fears another;
  the other arms more because this armament alarms it;
   each subsidizes a third and a fourth to aid it.
Two fight; all fight; none knows how to stop;
  a planet is stained red in the solidarity of hate and horror.

*O Lord, since first the blood of Abel*
*cried to you from the ground that drank it,*
*this earth of yours has been defiled*
*with the blood of man shed by his brother's hand,*
*and the centuries sob with the ceaseless horror of war.*
*Ever the pride of kings and the covetousness of the strong*
*has driven peaceful nations to slaughter.*

# Hate and War
## Luke 6:27-36

*To you who are listening to me I say,*
*Love your enemies, do good to those who hate you,*
*bless those who curse you.*
*Do you therefore be merciful,*
*as your Father is merciful.*
(verses 27-28, 36, Montgomery)

The Great War of 1914 has been
   the most extensive demonstration of the collapse of love
   which any of us wants to see.
As soon as one nation no longer recognizes
   the social unity with another nation,
      all morality collapses,
         and a deluge of hate, cruelty, and lies follow.
Hate breeds war and war breeds hate;
hate is expressed in willingness to believe evil
   and to publish lies, in fear, and in malice;
in this sense all the belligerent nations hate,
   and we stand alongside and hate for company's sake;
the effort to unload the blame on one party
   is unscientific, unjust, plugs up the intellect,
      and creates pharisaism.
We must all repent
   and remove the economic and moral causes of war.
Meanwhile, as individuals and as Christian churches,
   we must step out of the realm of hatred
   into the kingdom of love and peace.

*May we hate iniquity and hate nothing else.*
*May we love God and love all else.*

# A Prayer in Time of War, 1914

## I

O God, we call to you out of darkness.
The heavens are black with the storm-clouds of wrath.
A hail of death is cutting down the harvest of the ages.
We had hoped for an era of peace, and behold this war!

## II

We had trusted that the nations were moving with steady steps
toward human solidarity and love,
and behold, humanity is thrust back to savagery.
The spiritual achievements which generations toiled to build
are being swept away as by a flood.

## III

O Lord, our spirits are sick with pity for our brothers who die,
for the women widowed of their loves,
for the fatherless children,
for the unborn who will be seared
with the curse of fear in their mother's womb.
The sun of hope is darkened.
We stand before you numb and helpless.
We can do nothing but pray to you.

## IV

But, O God in whom our ancestors trusted,
today we pray with a purpose.
We ask for a miracle of your saving power.
Let not the end come by bleeding exhaustion
but by the stern protest of the people
and the righteous will of the leaders.
We know not how.
Therefore, we cry to you.

## V

Do wrest good out of evil.
Amid the clash of battle
build up the larger unity of nations.
Give freedom to the common person.
By the terror of this experience
confirm us all in a settled hate of war.
Dispel forever the lies and illusions
that have enchanted the mass.
Make bare your mighty arm.
Beat the sword and the cannon on the anvil of history
till they are forged into tools of peace
that will build up lasting institutions
of international justice and redress.

## VI

We beseech you to save our nation
from being sucked into the present flood of passion.
May our land remain an island of peace
in this red sea of trouble.
Grant our people a sober and neutral mind,
fair and friendly to all nations,
remembering our own sins,
and when the hour comes may our nation be fit
to serve all humanity
as the messenger of peace and the healer of wounds.

## VII

Our Father,
let your kingdom come
and your will be done on earth!
Forgive us our debts!
Deliver us from evil!

According to Rauschenbusch's handwritten note on the document, this prayer was published in *The Independent*, October 5, 1914. Copy located in ABHS Rauschenbusch Family Collection Box 26 Folder 15.

# Seek the Always-But-Coming Kingdom
## Matthew 6:25-34

*Continue to seek first God's kingdom and righteousness,
and all these things shall be added to you.*
(verse 33, Montgomery)

In asking for faith in the possibility of a new social order,
    we ask for no Utopian delusion.
We know well that there is no perfection
    for humanity in this life:
      there is only growth toward perfection....
We make it a duty to seek what is attainable....
We shall never have a perfect social life,
    yet we must seek it with faith.
We shall never abolish suffering.
    There will always be death and the empty chair and heart.
    There will always be the agony of love unreturned....
At best there is always but an approximation
    to a perfect social order.
The kingdom of God is always but coming.
    But every approximation to it is worthwhile.

*O Christ, may we not at the end of our years
bear the self-contempt of the coward,
nor the despair of those
who have sold their Master for silver,
but may we come to the gates of your city at last
with our sword still naked
and be worthy to walk before you
with all those whom the world had not cowed.*

# Poems and Hymns for Life with God in Solidarity

## Woodrow Wilson's Prayer

*A poem included in one of Rauschenbusch's scrapbooks.*

A nation deeply stirred by solemn passion
   At sight of wrong
Calls to heroic work of restoration
   The brave and strong.
With heartstrings swept as by an air from heaven—
   From God's white throne—
We listen to the moan of countless thousands,
   Life's undertone.
No day of triumph but of dedication
   Is this our time;
Men's hearts, men's lives, men's hopes appoint us
   Our task sublime.
O God, here at the hearthstone of the conscience
   We seek Thy light;
Justice, and only justice, is our motto—
   Show us the right!

William G. Ballantine, published title "An Inauguration." Ballantine commented, "These verses are made up almost entirely of phrases from the President's inaugural address." Copy in ABHS Rauschenbusch Family Collection, Box 28 Folder 3.

# "The Preacher's Mistake"

*A poem included in one of Rauschenbusch's scrapbooks.*

The parish priest of Austerity
Climbed up in a high church steeple,
To be nearer God so that he might hand
His word down to his people.

And in sermon script he daily wrote
What he thought was sent from heaven,
And he dropped this down on his people's heads,
Two times one day in seven.

And in his age God said, "Come down and die,"
And he cried from out the steeple,
"Where art thou, Lord?" And the Lord replied,
"Down here among my people."

William Doane (1832–1913), "The Preacher's Mistake," in Hazel Felleman and Edward Frank Allen, *The Best Loved Poems of the American People* (Doubleday, 1936).

# "For All the Saints"

*Sung on November 18, 1918, during the Rochester Theological Seminary memorial service for Walter Rauschenbusch.*

For all the saints
   who from their labors rest,
Who thee by faith
   before the world confessed,
Thy name, O Jesus,
   be forever blest:
Alleluia, Alleluia!

Thou wast their rock,
   their fortress, and their might;
Thou, Lord, their captain
   in the well-fought fight;
Thou, in the darkness
   still their one true light.
Alleluia, Alleluia!

O may thy soldiers,
   faithful, true, and bold,
Fight as the saints who
   nobly fought of old,
And win, with them,
   the victor's crown of gold.
Alleluia, Alleluia!

O blest communion,
   fellowship divine!
We feebly struggle,
   they in glory shine;
Yet all are one
   in thee, for all are thine.
Alleluia, Alleluia!

And when the strife
   is fierce, the warfare long,
Steals on the ear
   the distant triumphant song,
And hearts are brave
   again and arms are strong.
Alleluia, Alleluia!

The golden evening
   brightens in the west:
Soon, soon to faithful
   warriors comes their rest,
Sweet is the calm
   of paradise the blest.
Alleluia, Alleluia!

But lo! there breaks
   a still more glorious day;
The saints triumphant
   rise in bright array;
The King of glory
   passes on his way.
Alleluia, Alleluia!

From earth's wide bounds,
   from ocean's farthest coast,
Through heaven's gates
   Streams in the countless host,
Singing to Father,
   Son, and Holy Ghost.
Alleluia, Alleluia!

William Walsham How, "For All the Saints," 1864, *The Baptist Hymn Book* (London: Psalms and Hymns Trust, 1962), 403.

# Reflections on the Passion and Death of Jesus

# Jesus and the Social Movement
## Mark 10:32-34

*They were still on the road going up to Jerusalem, and Jesus led the way; and they were amazed, and some, although they followed, were afraid.*
(verse 32, Montgomery)

Who ever felt the worth of a soul more deeply than Jesus?
Who felt intenser pity for bodily disablement
   than he who touched the leper
   and quieted the demoniac's stormy soul?
Who had more of the spirit of real democracy
   than he who shared the fisherman's food,
   rebuked with dignity the haughty Pharisee
     who had failed in the common duties of hospitality,
   exalted the mite of the widow,
   and made his royal entry into the city of David
     on the back of a donkey,
       with boughs scattered by peasants as a carpet on the way?
Whose eye was ever quicker
   to detect the divine glory of a human heart
   beneath the rust and foulness of sin and social ostracism,
   than his who made friends with publicans…?
We cannot help feeling that the social movement was in Christ,
   and that Christ is now in the social movement.

*O Christ, our Lord, we turn back in these days*
*to meditate on your passion and death.*
*Grant us to see a new light on its mysteries and to gain a deeper insight*
*into the meaning of your life and death.*

# Capitalism and the Common Good
## Luke 19:45-48

*Then he went to the Temple and began to drive out the dealers.*
(verse 45, Montgomery)

Our capitalistic commerce and industry
  lies…as an unregenerate part of the social order,
    not based on freedom, love, and mutual service, as they are,
    but based on autocracy, antagonism of interests, and exploitation….
Life is holy.
Respect of life is Christian….
The life of great masses has been
  kept low by poverty,
  haunted by fear,
  and deprived of the joyous expression of life in play.
Beauty is a manifestation of God.
  Capitalism is ruthless of the beauty of nature
    if its sacrifice increases profit….
Devotion to the common good is one of the holy
  and divine forces in human society.
  Capitalism teaches us to set private interest
    before the common good….
To set Things above People
  is the really dangerous practical materialism.
To set Mammon before God
  is the only idolatry against which Jesus warned us.
The perpetual competitor of God is Mammon.

*Though the people hung upon your lips and learned of you*
*to serve the Father in the freedom of love,*
*the guardians of religion feared and hated you*
*as a destroyer of the Father's law.*

# Jesus, the Solidarist

## John 13:1-5

*Jesus, knowing that his hour had come when he should leave this world to go to the Father, having loved his own, who were in the world, showed forth his love to the end.*
(verse 1, Montgomery)

Jesus has no saying denouncing the poor....
He never called them "offspring of vipers."
He said, "Come unto me all ye that labor and are heavy laden."
    We are in the habit of appropriating that to our spiritual needs,
    but he may have thought of the hard working
    and heavy burdened people whom he saw all around him.
Jesus reverenced their power of love and sacrifice.
    It was a poor shepherd who went out after his lost sheep
        when he was tired at the end of the day;
    it was a poor woman who swept the whole house
        to find the lost coin.
    It was a poor widow who gave away her whole living.
Such actions spoke to his heart.
I think Jesus was frankly partisan on the side of the poor....
Jesus was a solidarist.

*Make us through your cross to know the love of God
who loved us to the uttermost.*

# Let Jesus Speak
## John 13:12-17

*So after he had washed their feet, and had put on his upper garments again, and taken his place, he said to them: "Do you understand what I have been doing to you?"*
(verse 12, Montgomery)

I feel that we must set Jesus free again.
We must let him say what he wants to say to us....
People have made Jesus a pivot of doctrine.
They needed his incarnation and death
  as the basis of redemption in theology,
but they have not always caught
  the tremendous social energy of righteousness
    which he embodied.
We are a little afraid of his teaching;
  it is so terribly incisive.
I am not afraid of the teachings of the Church....
But when it comes to the moral demands of Jesus
  I step out,
I am smitten with conviction of sin
  when he applies his standards to me.
The Church has not yet appropriated
  all the spiritual forces and values
    contained in the teachings of Jesus himself.

*Reveal to us through the cross the power of sin.*
*Make us realize the bitterness and vindictiveness of the sin*
*that struck at you and killed you,*
*that we may have no illusions about the conflict that is before us*
*if we too would fight sin and redeem the world.*

# Go in the Direction of the Master

## John 15:11-14

*Love one another just as I have loved you.*
(verse 12, Goodspeed)

The disciples of Jesus must follow their master,
  and they cannot follow him
  unless they go in the same direction.
By their attitude to this movement,
    more than by assent to formulated truths,
  will the disciples of our generation be judged before God.
"Once to every man and nation
  comes the moment to decide,
In the strife 'twixt truth and falsehood,
  for the good or evil side;
Some great cause, God's new Messiah,
  deals to each the bloom or blight,
Parts the goats upon the left hand
  and the sheep upon the right,
And the choice goes by forever
  'twixt that darkness and that light."

*Make us through your cross to know the love of God*
*who followed the lost sheep not only with bleeding feet,*
*but with bleeding hands and side and head,*
*yes, with bleeding heart.*

The quoted lyrics (in quotation marks) appear in a hymn, "Once to Every Man and Nation," based on James Russell Lowell's 1845 poem "The Present Crisis." See https://hymnary.org/text/once_to_every_man_and_nation.

# Law and Order
## Matthew 26:57-68

*And the chief priests and the whole Sanhedrin*
*were trying to get false evidence against Jesus,*
*in order that they might have him executed;*
*but they found none,*
*although many false witnesses came forward.*
(verses 59-60, Montgomery)

Law is unspeakably precious.
Order is the daughter of heaven.
Yet in practice law and order
  are on the side of those in possession.
Those who are out
  can get in
    only through the disturbance
    of the order now prevailing.
Those who in the past cried for law and order at any cost
  have throttled many a new-born child of justice.
The aristocracy and bureaucracy...are all for law and order,
  for law and order mean
    the old law and their own order.

*The people shouted for joy about the lowly pomp of your kingship,*
*hoping that their deliverance had come,*
*but the high court of your nation plotted your death*
*and found your gentle lips guilty of blaspheming God.*

# If, Then

## Matthew 26:69-75

*I never knew the man!*
(verse 74, Montgomery)

If there are statesmen, prophets, and apostles
   who set truth and justice above selfish advancement;
if their call finds a response in the great body of the people;
if a new tide of religious faith and moral enthusiasm
   creates new standards of duty
   and a new capacity for self-sacrifice;
if the strong learn to direct their love of power
   to the uplifting of the people
   and see the highest self-assertion in self-sacrifice—
then the intrenchments of vested wrong
   will melt away;
the stifled energy of the people
   will leap forward;
the atrophied members of the social body
   will be filled with a fresh flow of blood;
and a regenerate nation
   will look with the eyes of youth
   across the fields of the future.
With unanimous moral judgement
   humanity has always loved and exulted those
      who sacrificed their self-interest to the common welfare,
   and despised those who sold out the common good for private profit.
The cross of Christ stands for one principle of action;
   the bag of Judas stands for the other.

*O Christ, all the sin of the world was laid on you.*
*All the ancient wrongs that have ever borne down humanity,*
*converged upon you and spent their force upon you.*
*All the sins of humanity converged upon you to crush your life…*

This prayer continues by listing the sins in the following reflections.

# What It Comes Down To
## Mark 15:6-13

*They shouted furiously, "Crucify him!"*
(verse 13, Montgomery)

The kingdom of God, as Jesus teaches it, means
   the salvation of the social order
   and of all the members of the social order.
Jesus lived in a constant realization of God.
He lived in God,
   not occasionally as we sometimes do,
     but as a permanent thing.
God was the atmosphere of his life.
But he had an equally strong feeling for others
   as his sisters and brothers,
   and each feeling was the product of the other....
It ought to be thrilling for us to meet a human being.
Jesus had that realization of humanity in the highest degree....
Jesus loved them, one and all, as human beings.
He could appreciate human life in crowds, too;
He had social consciousness.
He had love—
   love, that is what it comes down to,
     the simple human instinct of love.

*All the sins of humanity converged upon you to crush your life—*
*...the fickleness of the people...*

# Economic Inequality and Political Equality
## John 19:1-16

*"If you release this man you are no friend of the Emperor."*
*So Pilate gave him over to be crucified.*
(verses 12, 16, Montgomery)

If we have a class which
   owns a large part of the national wealth
     and controls nearly all the mobile part of it,
  it is idle to suppose that this class will not see to it
    that the vast power exerted by the machinery of government
      serves its interests.
And if we have another class which
  is economically dependent and helpless,
    it is idle to suppose that it will be allowed
     an equal voice in swaying political power.
In short, we cannot join economic inequality and political equality....
To secure special concessions and privileges
  and to evade public burdens
    have always been the objects
      for which dominant classes used their political power.

*All the sins of humanity converged upon you to crush your life—*
*...the corruption of the powerful...*

# Yeasty with Privilege
## Mark 15:1-15

*Pilate recognized that it was through spite*
*that the high priests had handed Jesus over.*
*But the chief priests had incited the crowds*
*to have Barabbas released to them....*
*So Pilate,*
*who wished to make himself strong with the crowd,*
*released Barabbas to them,*
*and gave Jesus over for crucifixion, after he had scourged him.*
(verses 10-11, 15, Montgomery)

In reality our life is yeasty with special privilege.
Where have these huge fortunes grown
   in a single generation,
     if not from privilege?
"By their fruits you shall know them." [See Matthew 7:16.]
Do we pick the pumpkins of millionaires
   from the grape vine of equality?...
Our aristocracy has no titles.
But what's in a name?
It is power that works.
God's country begins where people love to serve their fellows.
The Devil's country begins where people eat people.

*All the sins of humanity converged upon you to crush your life—*
*...the timidity of the privileged...*

# Crossing Racial Boundary Lines, Outgrowing Nationalistic Religion
## Luke 23:6-12

*Herod began asking him many questions, but Jesus made no answers.*
*Meanwhile the high priests and Scribes were standing around,*
*and continually making accusations against him.*
(verses 9-10, Montgomery)

The God whom Jesus bore within him
   was not the God of one nation.
The reign of God which he meant to establish
   was not a new imperialism
     with the chosen people on the top of the pile.
The gospels show us Jesus in the act
   of crossing the racial boundary lines
   and outgrowing nationalistic religion.
He recognized the religious qualities of a pagan;
he foresaw that the kingdom of God
   would cut across the old lines of division;
he held up the hyphenated and heretical Samaritan
   as a model of humane kindness.
Every time a wider contact was offered him,
he seized it with a sense of exultation,
   like the discoverer of a new continent.
That world-wide consciousness of humanity,
   which is coming to some in protest
     against the hideous disruption and hatred of the War,
was won by Jesus at less cost under the tuition
   of God and the kingdom ideal.

*All the sins of humanity converged upon you to crush your life—*
*…the bigotry of the religious.*
*They all gathered as a dark cloud about your spirit*
*and caused you to cry to your father in loneliness of soul.*
*O Christ, forgive us,*
*for we, too, have often joined the spirit of those*
*who mocked and slew you.*

# Not Only Mercy, but Justice
## Colossians 2:15

*Principalities and power he disarmed, and openly displayed them as his trophies, when he triumphed over them in the cross.*
(Montgomery)

It is not good science to heal effects
   and say nothing of causes.
It is hardly incisive enough for those
   who speak the name of Christ
   to say that people ought to have a living wage.
When Jesus discussed ethical questions,
   he went with terrible directness at the heart of things.
The word of God is not traceable in surface scratches
   but is a two-edged sword that cuts to the marrow.
We want not only mercy, but justice.
We want not only social service,
   but social repentance, social shame,
   social conversion, and social regeneration....
Today the Lord is coming in social righteousness.

*O Christ, make your cross, that dark instrument of torture, the revealer of your glorious and eternal love for humanity.*

# Dare We?

## 1 Peter 2:21-25

*He bore our sins in his own body upon the tree,*
*in order that we might become dead to sins,*
*and be alive unto righteousness.*
(verse 24, Montgomery)

We hear the ends of the earth calling for social redemption.
The question is,
    dare we make an enlarged application
    of the Christian salvation
    to our modern conditions,
    which will be just as energetic and brave
    as what the Christians did in the early centuries
    under the difficult conditions and limitations
    in which they had to work?
Does the old prophetic spirit live in us?
Do we believe in the kingdom of God,
    in which God's will shall be done?
Shall we prepare the world for its coming?
    "Make ready the road before the Lord!
    Level the path before him!
    Every low place shall be filled up.
    Every mountain and hill shall be laid low.
    The crooked shall be made straight.
    The rough road shall be made smooth.
    So shall all flesh see the saving glory of the Lord." [See Isaiah 40:3-5.]

*O Christ, may your cross never be to us a device of theology,*
*but make it a power to awaken in us*
*a living passion for you and your service.*

# "Holy Fortitude"

## 1 Corinthians 16:13

*Be watchful, stand firm in faith, be courageous, be strong.*
(Montgomery)

*This Isaac Watts hymn was sung during the Rochester Theological Seminary memorial service for Walter Rauschenbusch on November 18, 1918.*

Am I a soldier of the cross,
A follower of the Lamb?
And shall I fear to own his cause,
Or blush to speak his name?

Must I be carried to the skies
On flowery beds of ease?
While others fought to win the prize,
And sailed through bloody seas?

Are there no foes for me to face?
Must I not stem the flood?
Is this vile world a friend to grace,
To help me on to God?

Sure I must fight, if I would reign;
Increase my courage, Lord!
I'll bear the toil, endure the pain,
Supported by thy word.

Thy saints, in all this glorious war,
Shall conquer, though they die;
They view this triumph from afar,
And seize it with their eye.

When that illustrious day shall rise,
And all thine armies shine
In robes of victory through the skies,
The glory shall be thine.

Isaac Watts wrote the poem "Holy Fortitude" in 1724 to follow a discourse on 1 Corinthians 16:13. In *The Hymnbook* (The Presbyterian Church in the United States, 1955), 353.

# Reflections on Thanksgiving

# "A Thanksgiving Meditation"

### I

Father, your child comes to thank you.
All this year your hand has been open
   to nourish me and mine.
We have never lacked the daily bread
   for which we prayed.
On the broad field of my life
   the furrows have been moistened by your rain
   and warmed by your sunshine
   and the harvest has ripened by your blessing.
When the blast of winter shook our house,
   my children were safe from the cold.
I thank you, Father.

### II

You have fed my heart with love.
Good people have given me their friendship.
The love of wife and child twines warm arms about me.
I gaze into bright young eyes, and bathing my soul in their joyous youth,
I renew my own.
The world is sown over with kindred spirits
   as the sky at night with stars.
   I need not pass through life as a lonely soul.
And all this love flows out from you.
Every brook on earth has its final source in the ocean of your fullness.
Every star in the heavens but reflects the light and glow
   that streams unceasingly from you,
   thou central Sun in the universe of love.

### III

You have built up my spirit in the knowledge of your truth.
You have supplied me with high thoughts
   through the Bible,
   through the hymns of the church,
   through noble books,
   and through the living word of those enlightened by you,

and my mind has seized them as the plant
seizes the soil with its rootlets
and draws nourishment from it.
There are truths of which I once had fleeting visions,
as of a far-off wander amid the morning mist;
now I have taken them by the hand
and brought them to my hearth to abide with me forever.
There are new truths now beckoning to me
   and my soul is stretching out its hands in greeting to them.
I shall have the joy of perpetual growth.
And to you I owe thanks for it all,
   thou great Educator of my spirit.

## IV

You have advanced me another year on the way of holiness.
My progress has been small, Father.
My eyes fill when I think of what it might have been.
Often I have stood still;
   often I have faltered and fallen.
When your call came to my ears,
   I was listening to near and seductive voices.
And yet I have come closer to you.
Some temptations have paled.
My unveiled soul has mirrored more clearly
   the glory of my Lord,
   and his image stands out more plainly.
Your efforts have not been wholly in vain.
I have denied you in the night of my cowardice,
   but my very sin has printed your seal
   more deeply on my soul,
   and my apostasy has taught me to whisper:
   "You know that I love you."
But it was only by your help.
If your strong hand had not drawn
   and lifted
   and upborne me,
   I should have perished in the darkness.
I thank you,
   thou Redeemer from sin.

## V

I thank you for your Holy Spirit.
When I was troubled and weary,
   your Comforter spoke to me.
When I was lonely and afraid,
   the great Companion was by me.
Amid the noises of the world,
      your Spirit's still, soft voice has reached me
      and has never let the homesickness die out within me.
As my heart pulses quietly and unceasingly in my breast,
and sends the nourishing red tide through all my body,
   so your Spirit pulses within my spirit
      and is the source of all holy aspirations within me.

## VI

I thank you for the moments
   when my life reached its climax during the year;
for the hours on the mountain-tops
   when the world lay before me bathed in your sunshine
   and heaven was open above me.
And I thank you too
—falteringly I thank you—
   for the valley of the shadow of death through which I passed,
   for there I learned to trust you wholly.
From the smitten rock of the desert
   flowed your living water.
My heaviest burden roused my highest strength.
I dare to thank you even for the cross you have laid upon me.
But remember, O Father, the weakness of your child.
Let him walk beside me
who bore the burden for us all,
   that in his fellowship
   my spirit may learn quietness and courage.

## VII

I thank you that you have given me an aim for my life
   in the great kingdom of Jesus Christ.
That all-embracing aim sets all my will on fire
   and unfetters all my powers.
To do your will is meat and drink to me.
If Christ, my Lord, had not set this aim before me,
   I should be seeking my aim in myself
   and my soul would grow narrow and dwarfed.
Now I grow with my growing purposes
   and your life runs at full tide
   when I pour out my life most freely for your kingdom.
I thank you,
   master of my labors,
   for your kingdom and my share in it.

## VIII

I thank you, O God of the coming years,
   for the hope that guides me on the march
   like a pillar of fire.
The consummation of life is waiting for me.
My life is not to ebb away like a brook in a desert,
   nor to be quenched in the smoke of age like a dying candle.
You will complete what you have begun.
You have implanted in me a life that is not of this world
   and will not perish with this world.
I shall live even though I die.
All that I have hoped and longed for
   shall be realized.
I am a child of eternity, and to you,
    Father of eternity,
     I give thanks for the living hope in me.

# Quotation Sources

## Primary Rauschenbusch Sources
### Books, Essays, Articles, Addresses

BC     Annual Session of the Baptist Congress 1887, 1888, 1889, 1892, 1893, 1913.

BOK     "The Brotherhood of the Kingdom," *Record of Christian Work* 13 (July 1894).

CM     "Christmas Message," *Life and Labor* 2, no. 12 (December 1912). Published by the National Women's Trade Union League.

CSQ     "The Church and Social Questions," in *Conservation of National Ideals* (New York: Fleming Revell, 1911. 99–122. See. https://archive.org/details/conservationnat00thomgoog.

CSC     *Christianity and the Social Crisis* (New York: Association Press, 1907).

CSL     "The Culture of the Spiritual Life," *Rochester Baptist Monthly*, November 1897. (Also ABHS RFC Box 63 File 2.)

CSO     *Christianizing the Social Order* (New York: Macmillan Co, 1912).

DWBC     *Dare We Be Christian?* (Boston: Pilgrim Press, 1914).

ISR     "The Ideals of Social Reformers," *The American Journal of Sociology* (January 9, 1896): 202–219. See https://archive.org/details/jstor-2761664.

NE     "The New Evangelism," *The Independent*, May 12, 1904. (Also ABHS RFC Box 26 Folder 15.)

PSA     *Prayers of the Social Awakening* (Boston: Pilgrim Press, 1910).

SB     "The Social Background, Spirit and Message of the Bible," *Rochester Theological Seminary Bulletin*: "The Record," November 1918, 54–63.

SCSM     "The Stake of the Church in the Social Movement," *American Journal of Sociology* 3 (1897): 8–33.

SPJ     *The Social Principles of Jesus* (New York: Grosset & Dunlap, 1916).

TM     "Thanksgiving Meditation," *The Baptist*, November 20, 1920.

TSG     *Theology for the Social Gospel* (New York: Macmillan, 1917).

REV     "Revelation: An Exposition," *The Biblical World*, August 1897. See https://archive.org/details/jstor-3140178.

WLL     "War and the Loss of Love," *The Standard*, August 26, 1916. (Also ABHS RFC Box 124 Folder 10.)

WAH    "War and Hate: A Reply," *The Standard*, November 18, 1916. (Also ABHS RFC Box 124 Folder 10.)

## Rauschenbusch Family Collection (RFC) at American Baptist Historical Society Archives

FS    "Funeral of D. Eisele" (Box 126, vol. 4:182–187).
FR    "Final Requests" (Box 129 Folder 3).
JOHN    Rochester Seminary Chapel Sermon on John 17:3 (Box 9 Folder 7).
MG    "Madam Guyon" manuscript (Box 9 Folder 12).
SSC    "Social Service and the Council" (Box 26 Folder 15).
PTY    Poetry (Box 12 Folder 9; Box 26 Folder 15; Box 28 Folder 3; Box 61 Folder 22).
PCSR    "The Place of the Church in Social Redemption" (Box 15 Folder 5).
PRS    Prayers (Box 26 Folder 15 and RTSB November 1918).
PRWR    Paul Rauschenbusch letter to WR (Box 120).
SJ    "The Spirit of Jesus," undated manuscript (Box 1 Folder 7).

## Secondary Sources

FY    *Rauschenbusch: The Formative Years*, Klaus Juergan Jordan (Valley Forge, PA: Judson Press, 1976).
RTSB    *Rochester Theological Seminary Bulletin*, "The Record," November 1918.
WR    *Walter Rauschenbusch*, Dores Robinson Sharpe (New York: Macmillan Co., 1942).

# Reflection References

The prayers used with each reflection are found in the Walter Rauschenbusch Family Collection at the American Baptist Historical Society archives, Box 26 Folder 15, unless otherwise referenced.

## Life with God in Solitude

| | |
|---|---:|
| The Castle of My Soul | WRFC box 26 file 15 |
| Soon the Silvery Light Will Rest on It All | SL |
| Haunted by Strange Shadowsq | REV |
| An Aid to Revelation | REV |
| All the Universe a Revelation of God | REV |
| Learn to Know God | CSO 125; REV |
| True Christianity | REV |
| The Writings of John | JOHN |
|     The Eternal Life | |
|     Eternal Life is New Life | |
|     Knowledge and the Eternal Life | |
|     Knowledge that Dominates Affections and Will | |
|     Turning Knowledge to Conviction | |
|     The Measure of the Eternal Life in Us | |
|     We Small Creatures Know God? | |
|     The Only God Whom We Can Know | |
|     Knowing Christ Is Knowing God | |
|     Eternal Life Pouring into Our Hearts | |
|     This is Indeed the Life Eternal | |
| Learn from Madame Guyon | MG |
|     Embrace the Good Thing | |
|     Restless Souls | |
|     Heartbeats | |
|     Seek, Yield, Be Open, Press Onward | |
|     Eternal Tendencies of the Soul | |
|     Not All of Christianity | |
|     It is Possible | |
|     There are Still Ardent Hearts | |
| A Power from the Unseen World | DWBC 11 |

| | |
|---|---|
| A Cry of Need | TSG 17; SCSM 32 |
| The Profoundest Classification of People | WR 272 |
| | (Rochester Baptist Monthly 1/1901) |
| A Strange Sweetness | WR 272 |
| | (RBM 1/1901) |
| The Ifs of Prayer | PSA 12,13 |
| A Breathing Space | PSA |
| Prayer and Morality | CSQ 121; WR 272 |
| Emotionless Spirituality is Valueless | BC 1893 |
| Talk Out as You Feel | BC 1893 |
| Reestablishing the Teaching of Jesus | SB |
| The Final Word for Christian Minds | SB |
| The Rarest Secret of All | CSO 47, 48 |
| Sharing the Secret | CSO 48 |
| The Deceitfulness of Riches | CSC 74 |
| Those Who Ridiculed Jesus | CSC 72, 73 |
| The Reign of Hate | WLL, WAH |
| What Hate Really Is | WAH |
| The Real Thing | CSO 63 |
| Keep Moving Forward | SSC |
| Taught What to See in the Bible | CSC 45 |
| Dear Mother…I Have to Believe What Is True | FY 12 |
| Dear Mother…I Cannot Do Otherwise | FY 12 |
| Dear Mother…I Am Stepping into Your Footsteps | FY 12 |
| Tell God Your Pains | FS |
| Present Illness and Final Requests | FR |
| Life is Still Worth Living | PRWR |
| Poems and Hymns for Life with God in Solitude | |
| The Hymns of the Church | RTSB |
| "Jerusalem, the Golden" | |
| "The Sands of Time Are Sinking" | |
| "Thanksgiving" | PTY Box 28 F3 |
| My Country | PTY Box 61 F22 |
| "Still, Still with Thee" | |

## Life with God in Service

| | |
|---|---|
| Inward and Outward | RTSB 51–53 |
| A New Feeling about Christ | |
| Urged to Give Up | |
| For the Lord Christ and the People | |

| | |
|---|---|
| Hold the Balance Even | ISR 219 |
| The Heart of Jesus's Heart | CSC 46, 48, 49 |
| A Fulcrum for God | CSO460 |
| Jesus Took Her Side | CSC 69 |
| Not Aristocratic Charity | SB |
| A New Avatar of Love | CSO 44 |
| The Prophets | CSC 41; 2, 3 |
| Heartbeats become Pulse-Throbs | CSC 22, 23 |
| Copying a Prophet | CSC 42 |
| If the Prophets Lived Today | CSC 41, 42 |
| The Worship God Demands | SB |
| The Mountain Was Still There | CSO 93 |
| From Future Gaze to Here and Now | CSC 64, 65 |
| The Kingdom Here and Now | BOK |
| To This Task We Dedicate Our Lives | BOK |
| For the Gospel to Have Power over an Age | NE |
| Pulpit and Social Questions | CSC 412, 413; BC 1892 |
| Church and Politics | CSQ |
| Preachers, Pastors, and Prophets | CSC 367 |
| Flowerpot Religion | CSC 26, 27 |
| Modern Christianity Not Christian Enough | ISR 202-219 |
| Protector of the Vulnerable | SB 56 |
| Wealth Is Timid of Change | CSC 413; BC 1893 |
| Christmas and the Cross | CM |
| Christmas and Purposeful Suffering | CM |
| The Corruption of Christmas | CSQ |
| A River Flowing from the Throne | ISR 202 |
| Divine Transformation of All Human Life | CSO 93 |
| Character and Community Transformation | BC 1889 |
| The Great Thing | ISR 217, 218 |
| Has the Church Lost Its Saltiness? | NE |
| Teaching of the Church and the Ethics of Jesus | CSC 314 |
| Has the Church Had Its Day? | PCSR |
| The Most Searching Test of the Church | SB |
| Christianized Commerce or Commercialized Church? | CSC 314, 315 |
| Make the Trial | CSC 342 |
| Blemishes on the Body of Christ | BOK |
| The Church Has Not Kept Pace | NE |
| Church and Money Power | BC 1893 |

| | |
|---|---|
| American Church in Hour of Trial | BC 1892 |
| Church: Help or Hindrance? | PCSR |
| The Spirit of Jesus | SJ |
| God's Pioneers are Always Few | CSO 373, 374 |
| The Church Is Where the Spirit Is | BC 1893 |
| The Most Daring Faith | CSC 415, 416 |
| New Apostolate in a New Harvest Time | CSC 414, 415 |
| Before We Pass Away | CSC xv |
| Poems and Hymns for Life with God in Service | |
| Hymns of Social Redemption | RTSB |
| "God Save America" | |
| "Pikes Peak" | |
| "God of the Nations, Near and Far" | |
| "When Wilt Thou Save the People?" | |
| A Responsive Prayer for All Who Labor | PRS 26.15 |
| "They Will Say" | PTY 28.3 |
| A Psalm of Great Cities | PTY 26.15 |
| "O Love that Wilt Not Let Me Go" | |

## Life with God in Solidarity

| | |
|---|---|
| "O God of Earth and Altar" | |
| History and the Dominant Classes | CSO 326, 327 |
| Speaking with Symbols | BC 1893 |
| Speaking of Salvation | BC 1893 |
| Whenever Jesus Looked | CSO 327, 328 |
| Does It Draw People Together? | CSC 70, 71 |
| God Looking at Us | SB 56 |
| The Sociable Jesus | CSC 69 |
| Our Business | SB 58 |
| Love Creates Fellowship | CSC 67, 68 |
| The principle and practice of koinonia | ISR |
| Putting Our Feet under the Same Table | CSC 69, 70 |
| The Gregarious Nature of Humanity | CSC 65, 66 |
| Bound Together | CSO 460, 461 |
| The Goodness Jesus Seeks | CSC 67 |
| The Highest Type of Goodness | CSC 67 |
| Systemic Affinity of Christianity | CSC 397; CSO 153 |
| Justice | CSC 110 |
| The Power of Public Opinion | CSC 260, 261 |
| The Reign of Fear Is Never the Reign of God | CSO 172, 173 |

| | |
|---|---|
| A Nation of Backsliders | CSO 151 |
| When Nations Die | CSO 332, 333 |
| The Abolition of Rank and Badges of Rank | CSC 87 |
| Unhorsing Privilege | CSO 334, 336, 337 |
| Private Interest and Chronic Corruption | CSO 280, 281 |
| Class Chasm | CSC 33 |
| Riches, Relations, and Renunciation | CSC 77 |
| The Charm and Curse of Riches | CSC 74, 75 |
| Economics and Politics | CSC 253, 254 |
| An Outrageous Betrayal of Justice | CSO 148 |
| De facto Emperor | CSC 262 |
| Forgive and Repair Torn Tissue | CSC 68 |
| Freedom: The Real Zest of Life | ISR 211, 212 |
| The Pronunciamento and Platform of Christianity | CSO 352, 353 |
| The Barrier Is Still Broad | ISR 207 |
| Open to All Who Will Come | BC 1888 |
| The Nerve of the Social Movement | ISR 203. 206, 207 |
| Shoulder to Shoulder | SSC |
| One Torch Kindling Hundreds | CSO 461, 462 |
| Let Us Counsel Patience | ISR 216-217 |
| The Process Is Never Complete | CSC 308, 309 |
| No Smooth Road | TSG 226, 278, 279 |
| A Solidarity of Hate and Horror | TSG 78, 79, 80/PSA 97 |
| Hate and War | SPJ 26; WAH |
| A Prayer in Time of War, 1914 | PTY 26.15 |
| Seek the Always-But-Coming Kingdom | CSC 420, 421 |
| Poems and Hymns for Life with God in Solidarity | |
| Woodrow Wilson's Prayer | PTY 28.3 |
| "The Preacher's Mistake" | PTY 26.15 |
| "For All the Saints" | |

## Reflections on the Passion and Death of Jesus

| | |
|---|---|
| Jesus and the Social Movement | ISR 207 |
| Capitalism and the Common Good | CSO 313, 314, 315 |
| Jesus, a Solidarist | SB 58 |
| Let Jesus Speak | SB 55 |
| Go in the Direction of the Master | ISR 207 |
| Law and Order | CSC 325 |
| If, Then | CSC 285; CSO 290 |
| What It Comes Down To | SB 56 |

| | |
|---|---:|
| Economic Inequality and Political Equality | CSC 254, 256 |
| Yeasty with Privilege | CSO 335, 290 |
|     Crossing Racial Boundary Lines, | |
| Outgrowing Religious Nationalism | TSG 161 |
| Not Only Mercy, but Justice | SSC |
| Dare We? | SB 63 |
| "Holy Fortitude" | |
| Reflections on Thanksgiving | TM |

www.ingramcontent.com/pod-product-compliance
Lightning Source LLC
Chambersburg PA
CBHW070842160426
43192CB00012B/2269